ROSEMARY BUDD

Rosemary Budd is a part-time teacher in English, history and religious education. She also leads workshops in the use of body and imagination in the development of the spiritual life, and her first book, *Moving Prayer*, is on this subject. She is interested in modern literature and writes fiction in her spare time.

Married with two daughters, she lives in Canterbury, Kent. Her particular aim is to encourage "a way of prayer which is powerful, contemplative and takes note of modern tensions and challenges."

SPIRE

Rosemary Budd

JOURNEY OF PRAYER

SPIRE

Copyright © 1989 by Rosemary Budd

First published in Great Britain 1989

Spire is an imprint of Hodder and Stoughton *Publishers*

Scripture quotations are taken from the New English Bible,
unless otherwise stated.

British Library Cataloguing in Publication Data

British Library Cataloguing in Publication Data

Budd, Rosemary
Journey of prayer.
1. Christian life. Meditation & prayer
I. Title
248.3

ISBN 0-340-50424-2

*Printed in Great Britain for Hodder and Stoughton Limited, Mill Road, Dunton
Green, Sevenoaks, Kent by Richard Clay Limited, Bungay, Suffolk. Photoset by
Rowland Phototypesetting Limited, Bury St Edmunds, Suffolk.*

Hodder and Stoughton Editorial Office: 47 Bedford Square, London WC1B 3DP.

For my father and my children,
in whose presence and absence
these experiences were forged,
and for my husband who travels
with me.

CONTENTS

PART ONE – BEGINNINGS

PART TWO – FURTHER IN

PART ONE

BEGINNINGS

INTRODUCTION

My father's eyes were blue: bright chinks of azure flashing merriment and pleasure; or pale screens behind which I glimpsed disapproval. Sometimes the blue burned me with ice-hot anger and, occasionally, it blinked wide in surprise. But always alive. Those eyes beaconed his vitality, and never more so than when he was laughing. Then he threw back his head with its mane of hair and beard and the flashing blue almost disappeared in a scatter of silver lines darting from the corners of his eyes like a shoal of little fishes. And my father laughed a lot. He laughed at people's jokes, and kindly at their foibles. He laughed at his own shortcomings. "What more can you expect from the son of an Irish immigrant?" he'd explain. And he laughed above all at stuffiness. Every day he took the train to work and joined the solemn procession of bowler-hatted city gents, umbrellas neatly furled, newspapers brandished at the ready to ward off intrusion and the chanced "Good morning" of the doggedly sociable. He found a friend on the train and together they invented a language. To while away the predictable journey with its predictable company, they chatted in "their" language. First a newspaper rustled and was dropped; then another and another. If, by the time the train pulled in to Liverpool station, the entire carriage was listening intently to them, my father announced he'd bagged a prize catch. Some days it didn't work, but often it did, and when he was successful I was first to know. "I heard one of them report that we were discussing the Russian economy," he told me one evening. "The man said he was quite sure it was that," he chuckled.

From when I was ten years old and first allowed to, I met my father at the station each evening. I hopped up and down, feet bobbing in impatience. Waiting; then he arrived. He bent his immensely tall frame down over me and, when the shadow of his bowler hat touched my forehead, I felt the first tickle of his bristly whiskers. It was like being taken under his protection: a small world bounded above by the brown bowler, in the front by the warm cloth of his city suit, and at the back by the stability of his broad hand pressed reassuringly over my shoulder blades. And, as I wriggled further into the safety his figure symbolised for me, he planted a kiss on the tip of my nose and asked, "How's my Sammy So Fat, then?" With the preliminaries over and my nose still wet from the kiss, he righted himself, took my small hand in his elegantly tapering fingers, and together we marched off for home.

We went on other walks together too. We lived about half a mile from the sea and, when the wind whipped the tang of brine into the house, my father put down his polished mahogany pipe, packing the tobacco in readiness for a relight later, slung his binoculars over his shoulder and invited, "Are you coming?"

It was enough to set me scampering for coat and gloves. Quickly, I pecked my long-suffering mother on the cheek (she stayed behind to cook lunch), half stroked the cat, and announced, "I'm ready."

As soon as we were out of the door, I slipped my fingers into my father's hand. "You never learn," he laughed at me when I had to loose him to get through the garden gate.

"No, I don't," I agreed defiantly, the fingers back safe in his hold.

I liked it best when the wind blew strongly. Then we faced into the gale, hair torn backwards, sand and spray pitting into face and eyes and the sea smell tanging our nostrils. Our clothes flapped against our bodies and my father's gold watch chain bounced and skidded over his leather waistcoat like a live thing. I watched as he tugged his coat to him, only its tail left to whip back into me and, arm in arm now, we struggled breathless, the cold stabbing into our lungs, hollowing us out, to one of the shelters. There we collapsed laughing on to the seat, glad we'd survived, pleased we'd made it so far. My father unwound his binoculars and scanned the shoreline. "Lots of red-shank today; a turnstone scuttling round as usual in the rock pool. They're such busy little things." The skin round my mouth thawed, my cheeks flamed and I got breath back, warm with pleasure as he pointed out more and more for me to notice. "Deadman's Pool's silting up and there's tufty grass out on the bank."

He passed the binoculars to me and, sure enough, there it was, a spiky shaving of green on the second bank out. "The tide's running swiftly today," I volunteered.

"Have you spotted the breakers out towards the Point?"

I swung the glasses to where white horses galloped in, tossing manes wildly in a sea spray of flecking foam.

Sometimes we talked about things – everything it seemed to me then. There was nothing I couldn't share with him. I told him about quarrels at school, and he slid an arm round my shoulders as he listened. He spun stories, weaving patterns of gold knights and silver ladies, and he gave silly answers to the even sillier riddles I tried out on him. He started to talk to me about growing up, and with the reassurance of that watch chain tickling my ear it didn't seem too terrifying.

I spent hours in the shed at the bottom of the garden watching my father make things. He designed and fashioned model yachts which we sailed when the sea was calm. He made one specially for me. We called her "Helen", and I learned how to furl and unfurl her sails, change the rigging according to the wind, and to race her.

When he was younger, he'd taken up calligraphy. I still have a verse of Rudyard Kipling's copied by him. It's illuminated in gold scrolls with a Tudor rose at the top and bottom of the lettering. A glass covering has protected it, and only the tip of one rose leaf has faded with the years.

He sang to me too. Often, after a bath at night, cocooned in an enormous towel, I climbed on his knee and begged, "'Mollie Malone' tonight please," or "'Had you but seen my Lady'."

One especially cold November evening when I was eleven and getting too big to sit on his knee, I snuggled by his side on the couch and, without waiting for me to tell him my choice, he started singing. His voice that night was unusually soft and gentle:

> Fear no more the heat o' the sun,
> Nor the furious winter's rages;
> Thou thy worldly task hast done,
> Home art gone, and ta'en thy wages . . .
>
> *William Shakespeare*

The words ached down the notes and, to still the ache, I pressed myself to him. The beating of his heart rattled against his ribcage; thud, thud, a long pause – then three quick beats together as if to catch up. It was not like the measured rhythm of my own heart-beats, and I looked up. The compassion which glowed from the depths of those blue eyes did little to avert the bolt of fear which ripped through my eleven-year-old security. "It's all right, Sammy So Fat," he whispered. But it wasn't. It wasn't.

After that began the succession of trips to the hospital. The ambulance roared up; men in dark blue uniforms strapped my father to a stretcher and carried him in. My mother, her face a white triangle of worry, climbed in beside him. A neighbour held my wrist firmly as I watched the white doors close. Had doors ever looked so bolted before? My fingers splayed open and I couldn't move. The neighbour's grip, like talons, dug into my flesh, and I knew that if I took one step it would be to start a breathless, helter-skelter, hot race against my fear and after that ambulance until I dropped. And it would do no good. There was nothing I could do. The ambulance turned the corner. I turned away.

We lived with my father in and out of hospital all that year. My mother grew thin and frightened and exhausted with looking after a semi-invalid, and I learned to creep around a silent house. In the September our cat died. That night I cried until the pillow grew hot and sodden with my tears. Long after I should have been asleep, how late I don't know, my father opened the door, shafting a chink of light into the anonymous dark of my bedroom. He held me close to him and my tears splashed onto the watch chain and dripped stains down the chamois waistcoat. "I loved Sooty. Why did God let it happen?" My sob choked in a small hiccup.

Very gently, my father held me away from him, his hands warm and steadying on my bare arms. He looked at me lovingly, so lovingly that it was almost unbearable, and held me until I stopped shaking. Then, with a strand of tear-damp hair still curled like a question mark over my cheek, I looked back at him. "There are some things you must not ask," he said, and the terror of being powerless scored my spirit again. But I knew he spoke the truth.

Autumn faded into winter and squeezed through Christmas into the bleak turn of the year. The ambulance arrived once more, and left for hospital bearing its precious cargo. After school I traipsed up the garden path as usual, my satchel beating time on my shoulder and my thoughts turning to supper, rang the bell and stood back when the door opened to reveal not my mother but the narrow, rather grey face of one of her friends. I glanced past her into the hall. Still no mother. Then a muffled sob escaped the confines of the sitting room. It wasn't all right, and I knew it. "What's wrong with Daddy?" I yelled.

The grey face winced, gathered its features together in a puckering about the nose, and told me in a small voice, "I'm afraid he's died, Darling."

"It's not true." My voice and my fists knotted into rejection.

"It is." The face unpuckered itself.

"Perhaps they're wrong."

"They have mirrors."

"What d'you mean?"

"Mirrors which they hold to see if the breath mists them."

"Oh." My understanding escaped on a sigh. No mist on the mirror. Nothing.

My father left me with a legacy of laughter and fun; poetry

and song; love shown in companionship and cuddles; and
eyes and ears that scanned the world and listened for its
heart-beat. His death left me with a legacy of loss.

For the next three years that loss arched over me,
cutting me off, draining my world of vitality and colour.
Life was probably far harder for my mother than for me.
She was still young, newly widowed and trying to cope
with going back to work. She kept the house as beautifully
as ever and made sure meals were on the table as regular
as clockwork. I was working for exams. So, for me, as for
her, there wasn't much energy left over to tell stories, to go
for long walks, to share secrets and to sing songs. Gradually the loss of intimacy settled like a pall on my personality
and I grew frightened and alone and very, very shy.
Absence wormed through me, gnawing bone and marrow.
It emptied my spirit of joy or trust or imagination and I
shrivelled under its onslaught.

One friend in particular tried to reach out to me.
Margaret and I had gone to secondary school at the same
time and, as we entered the fourth year, she was emerging
as a quiet, musical girl who sang in the school choir. We
shared a love of English and took it in turns to be class
representative at the Literary and Debating Society.

Margaret was shortish, whereas I was tall, she was fair
and I dark, so we must have looked ill-assorted as we
walked round the school field together at break times.
There was one other difference too. Margaret was a
Christian whereas I was not. I found out this alarmingly
embarrassing fact after one geography lesson. Our
geography teacher during this year was a young woman
fresh out of college who, at the best of times, seemed
uncertain of herself. She wore the then fashionable sun
ray pleated skirts and had a habit of punctuating her
teaching with, "Now, where was I?" She had a name but
we called her "Miss".

During one interminable summer's afternoon in the
classroom when the droning of a misdirected bumble bee
mingled with the droning of the lesson, one of the girls at
the side of the class stood up without warning, stretched

her arms wide above her head, yawned loudly so that I counted each one of the silver-grey fillings in her teeth, and then eased her cotton dress down over her sticky thighs. She grinned round, sat heavily and crossed her arms on the desk. In a shocked silence, we waited. The insensitive bee buzzed and zipped across a window searching for an opening. Miss stopped speaking; her jaw fell slackly open. Then she pulled it up sharply like a drawbridge and snapped, "How dare you, Jane Simmons! Don't you ever get up again without permission."

We breathed a sigh of relief. The world had been kept within bounds. Order was restored.

Miss turned to the blackboard, picked up her chalk and started to draw in the outline of South America. The shoulders of her cotton dress jiggled, sending the patterned sprays of rosebuds waving their leaves down her back. Then the entire back rounded, crouched and bent over. "What's up?" I whispered to Margaret.

"Don't know." Margaret sounded alarmed. Then "She's got an attack of the giggles."

"So she has."

The girls nearest us overheard and, with the rat-tat efficiency of a bush telegraph, the signal clicked and dotted throughout the entire class. "She's giggling. She can't stop."

Boundaries collapsed. We trampled order underfoot. No one took any notice of Miss for the rest of that lesson or for any of her further time with us. That is, no one except Margaret. While the class cavorted and trampled behind her to the accompaniment of banged desk lids, flicked paper darts and Miss' rusty wail of, "Really, 4B!" Margaret sat still in the front row. And that sitting fascinated me. She seemed calm and relaxed with an alert attention about her eyes and in the poise of her head. It was certainly not the sitting still of a class creep, toadying for favour when all about are losing theirs. There was nothing of condemnation or of pride in the straightness of her back, rather it was the absence of those which fascinated me. Her sitting struck me as a form of graciousness.

"Why d'you do it?" I asked after several weeks' observation.

"Because she's a person."

The answer mystified me. Weren't we all people? "What d'you mean?"

"She's in authority over us and we ought to respect her."

"That's not the same thing." I ambushed the inconsistency. Touching a raw spot in Margaret's argument soothed the discomfort her graciousness aroused in me. It was the first time I realised how cramped and mean sin is. It can't afford to be generous.

"Perhaps you're right," Margaret agreed. "But have you ever thought how she feels?"

I hadn't and I didn't want to then. "I won't be able to see you after all on Saturday." I terminated the conversation. I was, of course, trying to terminate much more.

Margaret hung on. The next time the topic cropped up, I asked why she thought she should respect authority. Her answer, "Because I'm a Christian", set spikes of irritation prickling into my spirit. The spikes dug and scoured and uncovered an increasing rage. Was she implying I wasn't a Christian? How dare she! What was a Christian anyway? How could she speak like that? Religion was a private matter and it had nothing to do with living. Living offered joy and the robbery of joy; love and uncertainty and pendulum swings of emotion whose arcs religion couldn't possibly track.

Margaret hung on. We took to walking home together, her measured, sure tread somehow keeping track of my erratic long-legged spurts. We swung out of school, paced past the rich men's houses at the top end of town, leapt from stone to stone on the path over the roundabout, narrowly avoided a bus as we crossed the road, and began the final leg down through the village.

The conversation turned to God. Margaret spoke to me about the love of God, and her words prodded my irritation to life again. "God loves us all," she told me. I raged at word and theory. We crossed the road. Almost at the end of the village now: almost home and I'd not have to listen to much more of this. "He can make a difference to you," she told me.

We passed the chemist's, and a sudden gust of wind tossed a flurry of dirt from the gutter up into my left eye. "Drat!" I foraged for a handkerchief, dragged it from my blazer pocket and fished the dirt away.

"He can make a difference," she insisted, "he really can."

My eye felt hot and inflamed. It hurt. We drew level with the fish and chips shop. The wind blew up from the sea bringing with it the tang of brine and its old, old invitation. But my father was not there. He could not respond to the invitation. No more walks together; no shared talks; no more laughter; no stories; no cuddles; no love. The anger in my eye and the anger in my spirit turned on Margaret. "God hasn't got arms," I accused and held myself tense and cheated against the wind. My nails bit into the palms of my hands.

She looked at me – her look, which was my father's look, clear and very kind.

As with him, I hesitated under so much acceptance. But I wanted it. So, like a baited fish, I squirmed on the hook. "God hasn't got arms," I shouted at her and the wind and God.

The hook held. With a voice as clear and firm as her eyes she assured me, "Yes he has, Rosemary. God's got arms. And he'll hold you."

In that encounter lay the seeds of my acceptance of God's love some months later. Perhaps my father's arms had, after all, been a preparation for and a staging post on the journey to the arms of my Heavenly Father.

God's arms held even when I wriggled and squirmed to escape. They didn't wrench or drag but, down to the finger-tips, remained pliant, open to me, beckoning. And gradually, the desire to escape receded. I snuggled down in love. Safe, I thought – home and safe.

God's arms flexed. Haltingly I started to realise that journeying, once begun, was not yet over. The arms enfolding me, enfold the universe and, within those still safe but vaster perimeters, I would be sent exploring and discovering, sometimes dancing, often limping, until I came to understand through a journey of prayer that God's arms are:

always satisfying and yet still drawing me
beckoning in pity and sending in joy
concerned fully with me and also with all they've created
   and are creating
pierced in grief and victorious over death
encircling those I love and stretching out through the
   galaxies and down the echoing years
cupped in offering and longing to receive
gentle as dawn light and powerful as lancing darkness
smitten in suffering and radiant with love
sometimes with a touch so delicate I interpret it as
   absence and sometimes so stable and firm it is like an
   oar's blade between my shoulders
raised in justice and girding in mercy
totally accepting and totally demanding.

And that God's arms move the arms of my brothers and sisters in Christ raised in worship, and of my brothers and sisters in Ethiopia extended in pleading. They move the arms of saints and the arms of sinners, of millionaires and of tramps, of the living and the dead. Nothing is beyond God's arms. They encompass what I like about myself and what I fear in myself, all that I have experienced and all that I will experience. And it is these arms which have sent me journeying, these arms which guide the journey and these arms which will be journey's end.

This book is written for all of us who wish to explore more fully such a continuing journey of prayer.

1

POINT OF DEPARTURE

Imprints of love

Why start out on a book about prayer with the story of my relationship with my father and a little of its place in bringing me to God?

For probably far more reasons than I realise: but, to name a few:

Firstly, and for me most uncomfortably, there's the question of prayer, and what I've experienced of prayer. These are certainly not the same thing. Prayer is much more than my experience of it so far. All relationship with God is personal and the fuller and healthier the relationship, the more it is just that – personal. So your relationship with God in prayer will not be the same as mine. Our Father's love is so imaginative and sensitive that he comes to each one of us in ways suited only to us. All we can ever do is encourage one another. All I can talk about is what I know.

And then, whatever we say about God, however we speak, it has to be in terms of our lives here and now. Jesus spoke like this all the time. He had grown up in a family with Joseph, a carpenter, as his father. His respect and admiration for Joseph must have been strong because he took on the family trade and became a carpenter himself. Later, in his teaching, when he wanted to show us how much God cares for each one of us, he used the family name: Father, God, our Father. The gospels are full of his stories explaining that God is like a father or, sometimes, a king, a judge or farmer. His kingdom is like a mustard seed or a pearl, and we are like lost coins, sheep, sons or young girls. So, we can only talk about our experience of

God in terms of our everyday lives. We say his grace flows
to us like a river; he moulds us as a potter moulds clay; he
forgives his people as a husband forgives an adulterous
wife.

Looking back to when I was a child, my relationship
with my own father seemed not only a preparation for my
relationship with God in prayer but also something of a
forerunner of it. As a child I learned a lot from my father. I
experienced his protection: when he was around I felt safe.
He opened up my imagination. He took me on journeys
into the past and, with him, the future held fewer terrors.
He was there to turn to whenever I wanted to share
laughter or tears. He led me on. And when the unknown
threatened, he came into the dark to be with me. But then
he too, for me, became the unknown. The security, the
safety and the dreams collapsed with his absence. Then,
from that death, newer life was born, life with a different
centre from my previous life, life with a different quality.

My experience of God has been a bit like that.

But, most important, the motif of those early years was
change and development – a travelling whether I liked it
or not. The travelling, as it turned out, was to be from love
to Love. I told the story for one reason more than any other
and that is because as a child, as a young adult, and now, I
continue to travel. I believe that it is in this continuing
search for fuller relationships that my experience is most
closely linked to all our experiences. We seem to be born to
search for something, whether we can name it or not; we
reach out all the time. In a sense, we are born to travel. But
is our restlessness a fault or a virtue? Why do we reach
out? And does this need to travel tell us anything about
God?

As I'm writing this my husband, David, is two floors
above me decorating one of the attics which is about to
become our elder daughter's bedroom. The way he works is
characteristic of him. He's been revving up to it for weeks,
assembling materials and planning when to do what. Now
he's got going, he can't start the day's work without a mug
of tea, and he needs further mugs at frequent intervals.

Equally essential is a fairly steady diet of Radio 4, sometimes punctuated by the explosions of Radio 1 as Catherine sneaks in to change the wavelength so she can hear this week's chart topper, "just one more time!"

Before he started David told me, "It'll take a week or ten days." I immediately doubled that and probably should have trebled it as friends are coming to stay and work will halt for their visit. Earlier today he dashed out calling, "Won't be a minute" and arrived home twenty minutes later flourishing a rasp which he'd discovered he needed for some of the woodwork. Each room collects one or two different specialist tools then hoarded away against future jobs like a squirrel's cache of extra tasty tit bits for the winter months. But unlike squirrels, David remembers where he's put things.

He's coated the chimney breast with three layers of an anti-damp preparation and he'll paste on a protective paper over that before he touches the top wallpaper. He does everything slowly, with the utmost care and planning. And when the room's finished, it'll be a beautiful job with gleaming paintwork, not a run in sight, wallpaper with no joins visible, a level and smooth ceiling where before there were cracks and bumps, and a co-ordination of colour that is so right that when I see it, I wonder how I could ever have suggested that the pink toned paper might look too sickly, or the darker carpet too dull. Anyone who pays attention to the end product of David's work could start to understand the character of David.

So too, I can look at the inbuilt movement we all have away from our isolation and towards others in the hope of finding love and trust, and catch in that an echo of the character of our Creator. As St. John declared in one of his letters, "God is love." (1 John 4:9) Love is God's name for his own moving out from and moving towards. Before God created anything, he is love. So there must be in God himself some moving out from and moving towards. That is what we mean when we describe God as Trinity. It's a way of saying that there's a relationship of love at the heart of the universe. The Father is always offering love to the Son, and this gift of love is the Son's glory, which he in turn perpetually offers to the Father, while the Spirit is the life of God electrifying the connection. God himself lives in a relationship of love and whatever he has created carries the imprint of this love within it. So our lives echo with a restlessness which is a longing for completion. It is the imprint of God in us which sends us travelling. Dimly we realise that there is no "I" without "You". We know that we are most ourselves when we accept love and when we give love. God's Spirit burns his imprint deeper into us, urging us towards more of the joys and more of the risk of loving.

We read in Exodus that God revealed himself to Moses and instructed him to lead the Israelites out of Egypt. Moses was worried by this and asked, "If I go to the Israelites and tell them that the God of their forefathers has sent me to them, and they ask me his name, what shall I say?" (Exodus 3:13) Many of our Bibles translate God's answer as "I am who I am." But a more accurate rendering would be, "I will be who I will be." The name of God implies the movement and creativity that is at the heart of his love. "I am" is static. "I am" has stopped. "I will be" gives us an insight into the eternal movement within God.

Not only is God creative love in himself, not only does this unstoppable love form the universe, but the love of God for what he has made is equally dynamic. God is always moving out from himself towards his creation and, with a graciousness which makes us gasp with wonder, strives to love you and me into a relationship with himself.

In God nothing ever stops and we live in a richness of creation. Sometimes we speak of creation as if it were solely an action in the past, like the winding up of a clock which now ticks away on its own. But it is God's Spirit who continually electrifies the connections which keep the universe in being. Because God is, we are: because God will be, we will be. He moves us into the future and towards himself. He creates us moment by moment. St. Paul spoke to the Greeks at Athens about this when he explained, ". . . in him we live and move, in him we exist."

And he reminded them that their own poets had said, "We are also his offspring." (Acts 17:28)

The focus of God's movement towards his creation is the man, Jesus. In Jesus God enters his creation; he identifies with it completely. It is when we are most in love that we say, "I am you." God's love is of that quality. It can bear no separation. In Jesus God's love sings across the galaxies and down the echoing years, "I am you." Jesus is the human heart of God. He is the heart of God travelling towards each one of us.

But Jesus' home was God. The gospels tell us he took time not only to speak to people, to teach and to heal, to receive and to give, but to pray. He prayed for his disciples; he prayed against evil and he prayed for future generations who, through the work of his disciples, would put their trust in him. But he also spent much time, whole nights we read, in prayer which the gospels don't tell us anything specific about at all. We read, he ". . . went up in the hills to pray" (Luke 9:28) or in Mark 6:46, "After taking leave of them, he went up the hillside to pray." Perhaps the key to what seems to be a "being" with God, a homing-in on his company for its own sake, is given us in John's gospel when Jesus says, "In truth, in very truth I tell you, the Son can do nothing by himself; he does only what he sees the Father doing: what the Father does, the Son does." (John 5:19) Jesus had no life independent of his Father and he needed time to be with God. In these times he burnished the family likeness of his Father in him. In Jesus the imprint of God's love burned through to the core of his life and then up and out to the rest of creation.

Jesus' love was attractive. He invited all to come to him: and they did. The blind, the lame, the diseased and the sad came. They were healed and sent away rejoicing. The confused came and were given meaning, and the bored received purpose.

But there was another coming, one which was different. In the last week of his life Mary came to Jesus with a pound of very expensive perfume. She spread the perfume over his feet and then gently wiped them with her hair.

She had not come to ask something of him; she had not
come displaying a specific need (although, like all of us,
she would have needs enough). She had not come even
wanting his friendship. She had come to offer and to be
with. What she offered was the perfume and her love. Both
cost her dearly. The perfume we find mentioned as being
very expensive, and her love led her to a public display of a
completely gracious act of humility and concern. She
lavished herself on Jesus, and in such a generosity of love
(no middle way here) she reflected something of the continual emptying out in love of Jesus towards his Father.
The lack of any quantifiable doing good or immediate
social benefit brought out the cries of "waste" and "shame"
that it so often has since. The disciples were indignant
when they saw it. "Why this waste?" they questioned, "It
could have been sold for a good sum and the money given
to the poor." (Matthew 26:8–9)

Jesus, who himself had been so concerned for the poor,
had made them the particular recipients of his gifts, his
teaching, his healing, his love, replied, "Why must you
make trouble for the woman? It is a fine thing she has done
for me." He added, "You have the poor among you always."
Jesus has not lost his bias towards the poor but he implies
that more important even than such a bias is the gift of
squandered love, a reckless generosity that is at the heart
of God himself. Jesus is not criticising working for social
justice, merely the cautious, niggling attitude of the cost-
effective approach to relationships which is so at odds with
the love of God. His rebuke is a reminder that efficiency is
no substitute for the eternal self-emptying of the love of
God which is mirrored in the beauty of Mary's giving.

The message is not, "Don't do."
The message is, "The quality of what you do can only
    reflect the quality of what you are."
In the end we have only ourselves to give.

The message is demonstrated even more clearly in Jesus'
visit to the house of Mary and Martha. Martha, like a good

hostess, bustled about preparing things for her guest and getting on with the household tasks. Mary dropped everything and went to sit at the feet of Jesus. This was definitely not what a well brought up Jewish woman was supposed to do. After a while Martha realised she'd been left on her own to do the work and, like lots of us when things don't seem fair, she appealed to the nearest authority to hand in an attempt to get him to swing his weight behind her case. So she complained to Jesus, "Lord, do you not care that my sister has left me to get on with the work by myself?" And without waiting for an answer, added indignantly, "Tell her to come and lend a hand." This was her equivalent of the disciples' case for a more obviously cost-effective use of resources. For Martha the grudge was based on the use of love and time and the distribution of labour. Perhaps she was not only surprised but disappointed by the reply she received.

Jesus answered, "Martha, Martha you are fretting and fussing about so many things; but one thing is necessary. The part that Mary has chosen is best; and it shall not be taken away from her." (Luke 10:40–42)

Again, it's not an either/or. Jesus does not dismiss the housework. What he does point out is that it is the quality of what you are which will affect everything that you do. There is only one thing which Jesus describes as necessary. He knew it was necessary because it was necessary in his own experience. Everything he did was part of what he was. Everything that he was depended on his being in God. His goodness was not his own – it was the goodness of the Father always offered to him and always received by him during those hours of prayer in which he enjoyed his relationship with his Father. Living, Jesus seems to be saying, is about a certain quality of being. It is quite the opposite of "never mind the quality, feel the width." Essentially, it is about abundance. And that abundance is realised by an entering into love.

Jesus is always beckoning us to "life ... in all its fullness." (John 10:10) This is a life of love received and love offered. Because we are all fired in the love of God, his

creative love is the hallmark of our humanity. Our longing for the depths of love is the craftsman's signature on
his craft.

"Come to me," said the Father to Jesus, and Jesus came
again and again. In the end he was able to say, "I am in the
Father and the Father in me."

In turn, Jesus and the Father invite us
Come to me
Come and see
Come and taste
Come and live
Come to me in prayer: not only in prayer for others and
    prayer for my world or my church: not only in prayer
    for your needs or in sorrow for your shortcomings
Come to me in the prayer of being with me
                        looking at me
Let me give you love for me
I will carve in you a capacity for me
Let me woo you, dare you?
Come
Set out on a journey.

Invitation to live

In late 1986 we moved from a bustling modern part of
Maidstone to the centre of Canterbury; from a place
of largely modern, utilitarian shops to rows and alleys of
hidden, secretive, backwater stores with a treasure house
of odds and ends, some of it trash but much of it worth the
rummaging. The architecture of the towns differs too.
Maidstone has an old foundation but its history has been
somewhat overlaid by unimaginative modern development. Canterbury has recently ploughed much time,
energy, planning and money into conservation of its
historic treasures. Consequently, walking through its
streets is rather a different experience from walking in
Maidstone. And, wherever you are, the Cathedral sits at

the centre of things like a loadstone, giving a direction to your steps and a gravitational pull to the whole city.

The day after we moved in both our daughters set out to explore. I was making lunch in the kitchen when they returned. "Mummy, Mummy," Susannah started her news before she'd got through the door.

I turned round, pan of peas in hand, it all sounded so urgent. She rushed in and slid to a breathless halt in front of me. "There's so much to see," she gasped.

"Oh yes," I damped things down. "Shops, houses, roads, people, just like Maidstone." I recited the list witheringly whilst draining the peas.

"No, not at all." Susannah's eyes glinted in impatience but she didn't give up. "No, there's a funny little shop with lots of different beads in its window, and we found somewhere up a narrow street and in through a door, a bit like a barn door. There are fenders in there. You and Daddy want one for upstairs, don't you? I'll take you there if you like."

That struck me as generous considering my wet squib of a response to her enthusiasm.

So, pan in hand, I looked at her. The pupils of her eyes had grown large and dark with the wonder of what she'd seen.

"Then there's a big church. It's enormous." She swathed a huge "O" with both arms through the steam rising from the peas. "We started to run round it, then we walked 'cause we wanted to look at the arches and the windows. It's just so big," she repeated. "And there's the ruins by it and the fudge shop, a knobbly tree and some china cats in a window, back a bit."

I laughed at the mix on the list, and Susannah busied herself pouring some orange juice for the meal. But throughout lunch she was quieter than usual and her eyes retained something of the afterglow of her looking.

Of course, she'd seen churches before, even a couple of cathedrals; we'd been round antique shops and she's always been able to sniff out fudge with the accuracy of a bloodhound on the trail. But this was different. This had

about it something of a "first", of a compulsion to look as
though what had previously been in the background of her
life had, that morning, swung to centre stage and had
pronounced itself THERE in a way which had not struck
her before. She'd been caught by the life of things in
themselves and her response was the open eyes of wonder.

Sometimes God's invitation to seek his face comes to us
like that. It's not that we've deliberately walked away
from him previously: in fact we may have been involved in
all kinds of church activity. It's just that he's been background to our work, the fuel for our work, his name often
on our lips, our prayers filled with Christian concerns but
we have not, as yet, been caught by his loving look. Then
one day, perhaps in the aftermath of some experience of
the presence of God in a meeting or when we're worship-
ping with others, we sense Jesus wants to give us a greater
sense of his presence when we're alone. The imprint of our
Creator has started to burn and irritate itself into our
lives.

Perhaps it isn't like that at all. Perhaps our experience
of human love is so rich that we question, "If our love can
be like this, what must the love of God be like?" And we
want to discover the fire from which all loves dart to us as
sparks.

Or it may be the opposite as it was with St. Francis of
Assisi. He couldn't get on with his father at all. It was a
question of Francis disappointing the rich cloth mer-
chant's hopes for him and, from Francis' point of view, his
father trying to squeeze him into a mould which he
no longer fitted. In other words, the Bernardone family
suffered from the crisis of a generation gap. One day, in
the market-place of the town where they lived, Francis
dramatically tore off the clothes he was wearing made
from his father's cloth. People quickly covered him with
blankets but they couldn't smother his words. He declared
that, from then on, he would turn only to his Father in
Heaven. Human love had disappointed him: there was
only God left.

Perhaps there are no such crises in our lives. We have a

reputation for fulfilling all our obligations with care and attention. Our lives are very busy, seemingly full and varied. But if we have a moment of inactivity, then we sense there's nothing there inside us, and the void is frightening. It's as if our activity props up our lives and once it's removed, we feel the threat of collapse.

Or it may be the contrary and we feel our faith restricts our life. We are sometimes torn to shreds with desires or fears which have no place in our faith but which are so much more real to us than our Christianity. We have ploughed on, imposing a scheme of behaviour on ourselves when our real life is leaping in our spirit in a variety of directions unfulfilled by what we say we believe. We speak of God but he seems to us small and claustrophobic compared with the vitality we feel inside ourselves.

It's quite possible, even as a Christian, to trail behind us the long disappointments of the years. These sap our energy, draining our life of vitality and colour until we creep like grey ghosts in a grey world. As the writer of Proverbs declared, "Hope deferred makes the heart sick." (Proverbs 13:12) What we'd daydreamed of acquiring in our life, even daydreams of acquiring spirituality, hasn't happened. And we're in danger of settling into a weariness of saying the right thing and doing some of the right things, with a life encased in lead when we'd hoped for a future glittering like gold.

It may be even more drastic. Perhaps there's a loss so great in our experience that we're hollowed out by it almost completely. Our world has come to an end: the ice has cracked and we've fallen through. If we're to reshape a world in any way at all then it has to be as a new creation with a new centre. There's nowhere else to go.

Maybe the loss has been less dramatic and we've experienced a gradual erosion of our lives so that we feel out of touch with people. We make a stab at getting to know them but real intimacy and warmth elude us. Our own need scares others off or scares us off ourselves and we come to believe that our capacity for love is frost bitten at the edges. People respect us and they may be kind enough but neither we nor they are at ease together. Once bustling lives are empty now and we rattle around in the echoes of our former usefulness.

Perhaps, instead, we have been suspecting for a while that there's something more God has for us and that our Christian experience is anaemic and parched, shrivelling almost before it's blossomed. Maybe we sense we're static when, in a way we couldn't talk about, we know we're meant to be moving into a deeper relationship. We feel that what is written in scripture is what we want but that so far we've hardly scratched the surface of living in Christ. For months I was plagued not only by the more obvious travelling words, ". . . thus we are transfigured into his likeness, from splendour to splendour" (2 Corinthians 3:18), but also by St. Paul's words in Colossians 1:24 when he says, "It is now my happiness to suffer for you. This is my way of helping to complete, in my poor human flesh, the full tale of Christ's afflictions still to be endured, for the sake of his body which is the church." The words sounded so dynamic. He talks of "helping to complete" and "still to be endured" and, so far, despite charismatic gifts, the Christian teaching I'd received had not unfolded much of that sort of journey. I felt I was on a treadmill of "more of the same" when St. Paul obviously moved further and further into his experience of the love of God and his relationships with other people.

If you're anything like me you both want and don't want such a journey towards Reality. Often, at a conscious level I think I thirst for God, but then I fritter my energies away on those inessentials that seem so vital at the time! So I set off on the highway and then ease off into a cul de sac or construct barriers to stay put behind. I long for God with a desire that pierces and then retreat into the safety of well-trodden routines and avoid a host of demands and difficult relationships such a desire brings with it. All I can muster is a wanting which is a half wanting and a hope which is partial hope. My running slows to a one step forward, two steps back stumble and I'm grateful to St. Augustine for his prayer, "Oh God make me chaste, but not yet."

I feel a touch of sympathy extended to me down the centuries.

You may not recognise yourself in any of these pictures. But whatever your circumstances are now, whatever your past, and however confused, dull, shredded, anxious or joyous you feel, the facts about what you experience and about what you have experienced are God's call to you, "Come". It is our dissatisfaction, whatever form it takes, which is God's voice. Our dissatisfaction is itself God's kindness prompting us to response.

No and yes

"Will you be coming to the party?"

"Yes. It's about 8.30 at your place, isn't it?"

"That's right."

"What shall I wear?"

"Come as you are."

That sort of conversation probably rings bells with us all. We've been told, "Come as you are" but I expect most of us haven't. We've rushed home to change instead. What we were wearing may have been acceptable to our hostess but it certainly wasn't to us.

If we want to come to God it's absolutely essential to come as we are – at least, as what we know ourselves to be. Discovering more of what we are is part of the journey. As God is Reality he can only love what is there. One of the ways we can remove ourselves from the love of God is by trying to present ourselves to him as we aren't. And often that's just what we try to do. God has no problems coping with our moods, peevishness or tantrums, let alone our restlessness, sterility or downright wickedness. It's we to whom such clothes aren't acceptable. So we feel the need to pretend we always wear Sunday best which is, of course, useless if we're hoping to enter into a deeper relationship with God who knows all about our weekday boiler suit, our off-duty sweatshirt and those much worn but well-hidden old clothes of our weaknesses and inconsistencies.

When I was small, the lady in the house next door to us

employed a cleaner who came in on Monday mornings to "go through" the main rooms. Our neighbour said she was worn out by the end of Sunday trying to get the place straight so that she wouldn't be ashamed to open the door to the cleaner on Monday! If we come to God not as we are but with the dust of our past lives consciously brushed under the carpet; the shadow of our envy, spite or ambition carefully concealed by lace curtains, then we are achieving only two things. Firstly, we are wearing ourselves out by all of that work – it would be easier on us if we didn't take the trouble to come at all. Secondly, we're making it almost impossible for ourselves to enter into the joy of the love of God. After all, we're far too busy putting up our own barriers of caution and acceptability to be able to receive the generosity of the love of God. So, our lips are saying, "Yes, I've come. Here I am" and much of the rest of us is playing games of not being there at all. Because we know God is good we've tried to align him only with what we feel is good about ourselves. Any such trying to prove ourselves acceptable to the love of God is a highly effective way of making ourselves absent from that love.

Jesus understood exactly how much we'd like to make ourselves acceptable to God – to be loved because we have proved we are worthy of love. But the love which we're worth would be a pitiable substitute for the love which God is longing to lavish on us. One of his most famous stories makes just this point. You can read it in Luke chapter 15:11–32. The spendthrift younger son goes off leaving the older son all the responsibility for being his father's right-hand man in the running of the estate. And this older brother fulfilled his obligations to the letter. He worked hard, was utterly reliable and, unlike his younger brother, didn't touch the inheritance that he'd come into when his father died.

Meanwhile, the good-for-nothing son ran through his inheritance money like wildfire, squandering it mainly on women. He ended up destitute and crawled home prepared to beg to be a servant in his father's house – at least they got board and lodging thrown in, which was better than starvation.

The father wasn't at all reasonable about this. Instead of waiting to hear the boy's abject apology and then setting him to work in a suitably humble position so that he'd be sure to learn his lesson and pay off his debt to the household, as soon as he caught a glimpse of him, he flung dignity to the winds. With a leaping of the heart he ran to meet him, flung his arms round him and kissed him.

Not put off by this display of affection, the younger son launched into what reads like a prepared speech, "Father, I have sinned against God and against you . . ." but it's as if his parent isn't even listening. The father hardly waits for him to finish but turns to the servants and puts into motion all the plans for a beanfeast of celebration and joy.

It is left to the elder son to be reasonable and to bring his common sense to bear on the homecoming. With a response that echoes Martha's complaint against Mary, he argues the case for a tit for tat sort of love, parading his record of virtue in front of his father. What's even more like us, he peevishly refuses to go into the house to join in the dancing and eating. It's an all too human response of cutting off your nose to spite your face.

This need to prove ourselves, to gain something to show how well we've done, in short, this need to bargain, is deep seated in human nature. It erupts every sales time when quite a few people, like me, buy something they don't need not because of the price it is now but because of the price it has been. What I'm grabbing, with all the acumen of the Irish peasant blood in my veins, is the reduction, not the object itself. The pride of the price knocked down in my favour gives the glow to the purchase.

We can be like that with God. What we all too often want is what we can think of as fair grace or, better still, cut price grace where we come out on the credit side. What horrifies us is free grace, especially if it's offered to someone we feel is undeserving. If something's free you can't put a price tag on it and then you don't know where you are. Ask yourself, if you passed a man sitting on the kerb offering £10 notes to passers-by, would you accept one? And, if you accepted it, could you bring yourself to fritter it away on something luxurious? If, like me, you'd be highly suspicious and embarrassed by such an offer, ask yourself why. Perhaps that gives us some insight to our reserve about free gifts. If I haven't earned a present, then what value can I put on my virtuous hard work (I'm so reliable and always do more than is asked)? What value can I put on my academic qualifications if I have any, or on everything I've saved up for so diligently over the years? The boat of my sense of who I am, and my evaluation of myself, is well and truly rocked. Our attempts to avoid love given freely are, deep down, attempts to hang on to who we are; to resist any kind of journeying out from ourselves towards another or others or God. If we can keep love reasonable, then we can survive it. We can also, incidentally, domesticate God, squeezing him into the image of our little penny-pinching half-loves.

But God's love wants to lavish, to run towards us, to pour out freely and to celebrate what he's creating. However diffident we are in coming to God, if it's to be a coming at all, we have to allow Our Father such a generosity. Cautious we may be, but we need to allow him to rejoice in us, not for anything we have carved out for ourselves but because we are his creation. As the Psalmist says:

> Lord, thou hast examined me and knowest me.
> Thou knowest all, whether I sit down or rise up;
> thou hast discerned my thoughts from afar.
> Thou hast traced my journey and my resting places,
> and art familiar with all my paths.

> (Psalm 139:1–3)

God is continually drawing us to himself in all that we experience. So we come, not trying to bargain with our own value or sense of fair play (and if we still feel compelled to flourish our credentials, then we might have the good grace to laugh at our stupidity). We come not grovelling in self-abasement, itself a sort of bargain – trying to be worthy by our display of repentance – remember the father in the story? He was far too busy rejoicing to listen to all that. We come as simply as possible. We come, as much as we can, as we are. We come to God in order to be there for him. We come with our past, our stupidities, our pettiness, our daydreams. And we come with our longings and our good points.

We come to be celebrated.

As an artist ponders the canvas in front of him and with painstaking care and attention applies himself to it and then rejoices in the expression of his work, so God rejoices in us, his creation.

Our Father has given us plenty of reassurances that he considers us worth such attention. We are told that, "In Christ he chose us before the world was founded." (Ephesians 1:4) In Isaiah 54:10 we read, ". . . my love shall be immovable and never fail." My favourite is also in Isaiah, the most perfect invitation, "Come, you who have no food, buy corn and eat; come and buy, not for money, not for a price. Why spend money and get what is not bread, why give the price of your labour and go unsatisfied?" (Isaiah 55:1–2)

We do not always find it easy to accept that God enjoys us but we can help ourselves to experience such acceptance by a simple exercise. Try this now – you may want to read very slowly and to pause from time to time to savour your experience.

Imagine you are standing alone with nothing particular to do. You're out of doors on grass that spreads itself luxuriously over hills in the background as well as under your feet. Sense the grass, its softness and sap-freshness. Smell the clean air. Look up to a bright sky and a sun that's pleasantly warm on your face but not too hot. Relaxing, isn't it?

Now imagine that Jesus comes to you. He looks at you. You've not been looked at that way before. His eyes are comprehending and very, very gentle. They bring your past into their sight and you know your future is safe in their reflection. The eyes look at you in love. The seeing accepts you, all of you, from your birth until now and beyond to the future you. The loving gaze accepts you as you are now. It asks no questions, it demands nothing.

"Come," Jesus invites. He takes your hand. You may find it difficult to believe he really wants you, or to cope with so much love. But the hand holds yours and you begin to relax. Together you walk through the grass. A single bird rushes its song into the warm air. A smile eases your mouth and then your eyes. You feel safe and happy.

Now you can see another figure. This figure is sitting. You hesitate but Jesus' hand is reassuring. You go on with him. "I have brought your child," Jesus tells his Father.

You stand in front of the figure. You don't know what to say. You try to mutter some words about the world's need. Your Father God shakes his head patiently and wisely.

You stop. What to say now? You start to tell him about someone you know.

He shakes his head.

You're puzzled.

"Come to me," says the Father. "Be with me. You can talk if you want to but tell me about yourself."

Jesus' hand is strong over yours. He leads you forward. The Father's arms circle round you. The arms hold you. You are accepted by them. The hold tells you that he loves you. His arms around you help you to feel that you were created for his pleasure. He loves loving you. He wants you to know that he enjoys you. And he wants you to enjoy him. All this is his gift to you. You relax into the arms. This is what you were born for. It feels good.

Now God looks lovingly at you. He speaks your name. You have never heard your name spoken with such gentleness before, not like this. God delights in you.

Look up at him. Let him enjoy you. It's the biggest "Thank you" you can ever give him. It's the most you can do for him.

> Lord of love and generosity
> Lead us to receive your love
> Help us to trust your generosity.

2

STARTING OUT

In prayer, as in life, the starting point is not ourselves but God. It is his Spirit who, through circumstances and our own temperaments, is always encouraging us to be there for him.

We cannot avoid having preconceptions about prayer and, like all preconceptions, they construct a firm foundation for our practice. But they can confine as well as build. The generosity of God may be calling us to a fresh creativity in our relationship with him. This will, in turn, broaden our experience of prayer.

Creativity takes time. Relationships take time. It's not helpful to think that our relationship with God is any different. If we're not prepared to give it time, then it won't grow. This may mean that we have to cut something else out of our lives but as the old saying goes, "There's always time to do what you really want." I'm not thinking of a definite amount of time every day, but I am suggesting that the love and creativity we call prayer cannot grow without nurturing.

Perhaps too, we need to take a long, hard look at how we prepare ourselves for prayer. The fact that we can call our Father, "Daddy" (the English equivalent of the Aramaic "Abba" which Jesus used) doesn't mean that a sense of ease and acceptance should stifle our desire to create the best possible conditions in which a deeper relationship can root itself. Love is not the same as carelessness and it is no excuse for it. Rather the opposite: the greater the love, the greater the care. Think of a time when you were really looking forward to meeting someone. Now, reflect on the preparations you made for that meeting.

Your preparations will not have been the same as

anyone else's. I sometimes wonder if we find prayer more difficult than we need because we try to impose other people's preparations for prayer on ourselves. We are all unique. A computer is marvellous as a computer and not because it's the first unfurling of a rosebud. The beauty we find in the intricate pattern of a snowflake is entirely different from the clean, swift cut of a well-honed sword blade. I repeat, we are all different, and part of our human responsibility is to explore the ways in which our uniqueness can work for us as a preparation for being there for God.

Perhaps we've been given an invaluable early training in reading the Bible using prepared notes or with a leader guiding us through a passage. The only drawback to this sort of reading as a preparation for prayer is the inhibitions it imposes on us. Firstly, we're required to "get through" a certain amount of scripture at each sitting, then we're directed by someone else's insights and, finally, this is only one, highly specialised sort of reading depending greatly on analytical abilities. What I've outlined won't be experienced as inhibitions by you if such a method of reading suits you. If you slip into it as a hand slips into a well-worn glove then you'd be wise not to discard it for some new garment. However, there may be some for whom the fit has been neither exact nor comfortable, or who are willing to tuck a few more pairs of gloves into their wardrobes. We may want to go more slowly or more quickly, to mull over things or to include more of our God-given imaginative powers when we read. If so, we're not only perfectly at liberty under the Spirit to try out different methods of reading but we're called to enter such a liberty. True freedom is like the freedom of God: it lies in the ability to be what we are.

There are many ways we can touch more fully on the possibilities open to us when reading the Bible or when preparing our bodies, as well as our senses, for prayer. As you follow the leading of the Holy Spirit, you'll discover much for yourself; you won't need anyone else's ideas or experience. So, forgive me if I just indicate some alternatives here. They'll read rather more like signposts than like the detailed information of a guide book.

Reading the Bible

If you're the sort of person who finds he mulls over the contents of a conversation long after it's over, or if you'd like to be more reflective, then a meditative approach may suit you. One of my friends spent some time mulling over the encouragement from Hebrews "Let brotherly love continue." (ch. 13:1 – Revised Standard Version) She reflected on the words as she was trundling her toddler to playgroup each morning. She asked the Holy Spirit to help her pan the gold from each word. She said the biggest surprise came with "let". She started to discover that letting isn't a passive "Oh well, I don't care if it's like that" response at all but more the sense of "allow". Even "allow" can be passive. Perhaps one of the children asks, "Are we allowed out to play?" and all we have to give is a preoccupied, brief nod without looking up and, in a flash, they're off. But we also use "allow" in the sort of sentence which reads, "They mined a tunnel through the mountain to allow the train to pass through." Here, allowing is the product of months of sweat and labour! So, she began to ponder on the ways she might labour to bring about conditions in her church where brotherly love could continue. She told me that it took the best part of two months to mull over the whole phrase.

Others find that just one word like "joy" or "compassion" will preoccupy them for days at a time. Again, there may be a period when we "nibble" at scripture, biting off one verse or phrase to return to several times a day.

You may have a restless, pell mell sort of mind, in which case a rather more rapid style of reading would be suitable. Perhaps you're happy with two or three chapters of the narrative sections of the Bible at a time. When you're on your own there's no one to accuse you of skating and dashing over the contents as if you're whirling on thin ice.

Perhaps a thematic approach suits you well, especially

if your job is to do with sorting or filing. Then it's possible to work through parts of scripture tracing the varied use and meanings of an important thread like "sacrifice" or "kingdom".

However varied the speed, these approaches are still fairly analytical. Principally, they depend on us thinking our way into the words. I'm convinced that all of us have more imaginative powers than we suspect and that we should use these also when reading. Jesus' stories are a vivid testament to his creative imagination. Under the guidance of the Holy Spirit your imagination can bring much to light that has remained hidden under the cloak of the analytical mind. This is perhaps why Jesus' parables were designed to speak to his hearers' imaginations. Sometimes our imagination speaks much more truly than our lips. We all know how we can say one thing and think another; how much more can we say one thing and feel another – even feel it at depths which we try not to acknowledge but which affect all of our life? Such depths are the sources both of psychosomatic illnesses and of the thumbscrews, racks and instruments of torment with which we compress and wound our capacity for joy. If we want to gain a little insight into how we really feel about Jesus having anything to do with us, then we could enter into an imaginative exercise in which we are at an occasion of great happiness.

Let us go back in our life to a time of joy. Now let us picture Jesus with us in that happiness. Does he really fit in here? Does he want us to be happy?

You can read of Jesus' reaction to an occasion of great human happiness in John 2:7–11.

Once you've become aware that your Jesus wants you to get the most out of life and doesn't disapprove of you enjoying yourself, then you can start using your imagination in other ways when reading scripture. Try turning to a Psalm and noting down the names of God that the Psalmist used to express a little of what the Lord meant to him. I turned to Psalm 24 and found "Saviour", "God of Jacob", "King of Glory" and "Lord of Hosts". Now add

some names of your own for God expressing something of
what he means to you or what he has done for you. It's
beautiful to offer the Lord the gift of a new name.

Let's return to the gospels. Imagine the risen Jesus
standing in front of you looking at you with all that
acceptance and delight that is so difficult to cope with.
Perhaps by now you're becoming more used to being
enjoyed by God. Now look up one of the questions that
Jesus asks in the gospels. Imagine him asking the
question of you:

"Do you love me?"
"Do you want to be cured?"
"What do you want me to do for you?"

Listen to the question carefully. Let Jesus ask it two or
three times. Then, answer it if you can. Sometimes I can't
form an answer. So I just sit under the question asked, in
acceptance and love. The Holy Spirit will lead me to
answer when I am able.

Again, you may be able to take one of the names of the
Lord in scripture and to "picture" the name. You do this by
imagining the name written in the air in front of you. It is
covered by your hands drawn across it like a curtain. You
place your hands in front of you, fingers pointing up, palms
facing out. Then, slowly, draw back the curtains of your
fingers to reveal the name. What colour is it? Colour is
important in scripture and the Spirit can teach us some
more about Jesus through the colours we associate with
his name.

As you become more accustomed to using your imagination you'll find you can extend the exercises to encompass
stories you read in the gospels. Let's take the example of
Jesus feeding the crowds after he's been teaching them.
You can read an account of this in Mark 6:34–44. Imagine
you're there in the crowd . . .

Why have you come? Have you taken a day off work? Are
you escaping from the situation at home? Are you here to
take your mind off a row with your wife? Should you be

somewhere else? Did you just drift with the general direction of the crowd, getting added on to it like a speck of fluff
clinging to some worn clothing? Why are you here?

How are you feeling? How many hours have you been
here? Are you standing? Have people trodden on your
toes? How dusty and footsore are you? And thirsty? What
does it smell like? Hot and fetid with the heat of a crowd
gathered during the best part of the day? How much could
you hear? Come to that, how much did you listen? What
are you thinking about, dreaming about? What do you
want out of life? Are you hemmed in? . . . You're hungry.
So are other people. You've been here longer than you'd
reckoned on. One or two stomachs are beginning to roll
and grumble their emptiness. You think you'd better set
off home. But you haven't got the energy. You're too tired
and ravenous. Those words which sounded so good a while
ago, that teaching, are lost in the emptiness of your inside.

What's happening? The man who was speaking, the one
they call Jesus, has stopped. He's conferring with his
friends. You recognise them; they're the men who are
always with him. There seems to be some sort of discussion
going on. Now he's stooping down to chat with someone
you can't make out. There's a strange hush developing. It
gathers itself round Jesus but ripples out into the crowd, a
sort of expectancy. He's blessing something in the tra-
ditional manner. Perhaps he's going to eat . . . You hardly
dare think of food. It makes your mouth water and your
thoughts scrunch together into a tight knot of desire. You
close your eyes and catch a vision of small fish spitted over
a fire. Oh that smell! Someone's bumped into you. You
blink open hot eyelids. There's a sway of the crowd
towards you like the building of a wave before the wind on
Galilee. They're parting to make way for one of Jesus'
friends and that means they're backing into you and
jolting you. The disciple walks into the path opening in
front of him. What's he doing? He looks as if he's handing
things out. You catch sight of a piece of bread and a little

fish . . . Some of it's being passed along your row. You hold
out your hand and take it. You've got a couple of fish – nice
and fresh they are – and a piece of bread. You parcel the
bread round the fish and start to eat. All around you people
are doing the same. But you don't notice. You're too
famished for that. All that matters is the trickle of flavour
over your tongue and the stilling of the clamour in your
stomach.

You've finished You look around. Others are finishing too.
The ground's a bit messy with all the crumbs. You feel so
much better; comfortable, almost human again. Speaking
of being human, how on earth did this happen?

Look up Yes, how? How? . . . And why? . . . And, most
important, who? Who is this Jesus who makes so much
from so little?

Look at him How does he do it? Why does he do it? Who is
he? What more does he have to give you? Why does he
always give? Is this a new way of living? How often have
you received such a gift before? . . . How long will you
think about this? A meal for thousands from almost
nothing? . . . How will you live the rest of your life now this
has happened to you? . . .

Sometimes when you re-enact stories or parables in scripture you may be surprised at how you feel. Perhaps you
astonish yourself by discovering you have sympathy with
the jeering crowd or with a Pharisee, or the inability to
respond of the rich young man when Jesus told him, "Give
everything you have to the poor." God can cope with
whatever you feel. It is only as we discover our responses,
negative as well as positive, that we can bring them to God
for healing. He can only satisfy our emptiness when we
bring it to him. If we place ourselves under the guidance of
the Holy Spirit we can explore an imaginative reading of
scripture without fear. God loves us and does not want us
to be overwhelmed by our own negativity. We may also be

surprised by sudden upsurges of joy or gratitude, which we
hadn't realised we felt, as our love for God flexes into life.

I often find it helpful to prepare for silence before the
Lord by the use of some set prayer such as the "Our
Father". I try to say the prayer slowly and with attention.
If my attention has strayed then I repeat the word or
phrase until I can do so with full attention. Gradually the
stillness needed to be with God is developed under the
words.

Use of the senses

If you're musical you may want to prepare for prayer by
singing or by listening to a piece of music with the same
care that you want to lavish on God.

Maybe you love colour or texture and find the doors of
shops selling materials a constant invitation. Or possibly
it's line and form and you enjoy pictures. Lots of us can't
resist the smell of freshly baked bread, nor its marvellous
texture – crusty and firm on the outside with a soft,
springy centre – at its best when still warm.

Scripture is full of references to materials, bread, wine,
meats, olives, milk and so on as well as innumerable
occasions of singing and playing musical instruments (no
wonder David, who'd strummed on his harp as a shepherd
boy and then soothed King Saul's bad spirits, turned his
experience of God into the poetic songs we call Psalms).
Nevertheless, I'd been a Christian for years before I
started to wake up to the presence of God in these things,
before I started to touch, to look at, to handle, smell or
listen with attention. I might equally say, before I started
to understand that everything is alive because God is
alive. It doesn't matter that we're also talking about
"unalive" things like material or machinery or furniture,
they are created by us and all our creativity is a tiny spark
from the furnace of the creative love of God which makes
and makes and makes.

God's world

God can speak to us through his world, through everyday
objects or the scenery we pass on our way to work. All this
can help us to develop the gratitude, receptivity and
attention that will allow us to enjoy God's presence when
we pray.

Not many weeks ago a small river running through the
city "caught" me just as so much else in the place had
caught Susannah earlier. I was walking back home after
work, tired and quite cold, when I was attracted first by its
sound, a spate of small rushes which, although quite quick
in themselves, came across contained in a long, soft note,
more or less unchanging. When I got to the bridge crossing
the stream and looked down, the sight of the water was
just like its sound. It rushed by, white flecked over rocks or
in whirls of grey-green in the deeper parts. But, as it kept
coming, it was impossible to divide it in any way – all those
smaller swirls held in the completion of an ongoing movement. My response to the river deepened as I looked. I
found myself reflecting on the constant change in our
lives, all the froth over rocks and swirls of grey and green.
But somehow, everything is held in the love of God as the
eddies of water are held in the total movement.

Then there was the movement itself . . . As a person I am
not something static. Because God has made me like
himself, I am only me when I'm going out of myself in
relationship. I am only me when I risk giving myself away.

There was something in the water also about time, past,
present and future, undivided as the water was always
changing but undivided. We are born from what has gone
before and we form a bridge to the future, to the third and
fourth generations as the Bible puts it.

There was something there about God, too, always
moving yet always complete. God's activity is a flow which
I can see in part but can't chart fully.

Along with all this there was the river itself. It sang its
own song, followed its own way and was there before I
looked at it. In a few minutes I'd leave and it would still be

there. God related to me through the river as something
there in itself. I am part of God's creation, made to respect
the individuality of all of that creation. The river doesn't
exist for me to influence it or to try to make it like me. (And
how often do I behave like that with other people?) It has
its own place. I had a sense of everything in the universe
having its own place, praising God together without one
thing bossing another, molesting or coercing.

This sort of looking is what the Bible calls wonder. It is a
looking without trying to influence. It is a looking in
praise. I was only on the bridge over the river for two or
three minutes but the quality of the experience put me in
touch with the sort of life lived in the wholeness that Jesus
spoke of when he said, "I have come that men may have
life, and may have it in all its fullness." (John 10:10) Such
wonder is the opposite of greed. Yet it seems that the less
we try to control the more we are surprised by a sense of
relationship in the universe.

We don't have to wait to be "caught" by experiences
either. We can teach ourselves to be more wonder-ful. All
we have to do is to respond to the way God made us. Try
this. Take an everyday object, like a piece of fruit or your
pen. Handle the object, pay attention to the feel of it, smell
it, look at it in detail and with appreciation. Finally,
imagine the Lord standing near you and looking at you
and the object you are holding. He looks with love both at
it and at you. Now look at the object again. How has your
attitude towards it changed?

Perhaps you enjoy trees. Then take just two or three
minutes to stand in front of a tree and allow it to be itself
for you. Run your finger down its bark, touch the leaves,
marvel at the intricate pattern of the branches. Allow the
tree to speak to you of its past, of the sapling it was, its first
blossoming and spring. What of its future? Of the passing
of the seasons? Praise Jesus Christ in whom and by whom
and for whom everything that is, was made. Thank God for
that tree.

Often it's necessary to exert ourselves over nature but
when it isn't necessary, the less we exert ourselves over

the natural world, but work to increase our appreciation of it, the more we become aware of a kind of connection in everything. That connection is God. As the Psalmist sings out:

> Thou hast spread out the heavens like a tent
> and on their waters laid the beams of thy pavilion;
> who takest the clouds for thy chariot,
> riding on the wings of the wind;
> who makest the winds thy messengers
> and flames of fire thy servants;
>
> (Psalm 104:2–4)

As we start to become aware of connections so we open ourselves to wonder at the creative love of God. This is why Jesus told his listeners to look with wonder on the lilies of the field.

The body at prayer

We can't prepare ourselves to be there for God without preparing our bodies as well. Your body is you and your body can be involved in many ways in the reading you do before you pray. Much of the Bible is written rhythmically and it responds well to being read rhythmically. Take a short sentence such as "praise the Lord" or "our God is mighty" and clap the rhythm of the words into your spirit.

Once your body's imagination is prodded out of its torpor you can use your hands to express the experiences of scripture. Several passages are suitable for this. Let's just try with a few words from Romans 8:35. St. Paul is proclaiming that nothing can separate us from the love of Christ: he asks, "Can affliction or hardship?" As you read, let one hand symbolise affliction. Perhaps the hand splays open in pain or curls in protection. Then try hardship. Maybe your hand bows under the weight of living. When I use my hands to act out the words of scripture, I find increasingly that the Holy Spirit brings associated images into my mind to focus on those words. The "afflicted" hands of a starving Ethiopian mother I'd seen on TV curled round in defence of her underdeveloped, listless baby, or with "hardship" the knuckles of old people crippled by arthritis. So, again, connections are formed. We come to God as human beings, so our relations with others are intermingled with our relations with God. As St. John says, "If he does not love the brother whom he has seen, it cannot be that he loves God whom he has not seen." (1 John 4:19)

We can also harness our bodily energy by walking when we are reading. The measured rhythm of our steps can aid the concentration and receptivity needed to take in God's words.

Perhaps we find a certain posture helpful when it comes to prayer itself. If you look in scripture you will see that people lie flat, kneel, stand, bow and sometimes even sit for prayer.

What about your hands? They can be part of your welcome to God. A slow gesture outwards with the palm up says "I trust you"; cradled hands can make a seat for the presence of the Lord. Part of our preparation for prayer is to learn to enjoy expressing our longing for God in our position and movements.

Perhaps the ideal would be to combine meditative and imaginative reading of scripture, a response of wonder to our world and the use of our bodies in prayer. But we're all different and God's Spirit draws us to respond differently at different times in our lives. So you will probably find that you are attracted to one way at one time rather than another. It may be helpful to bear in mind that if one approach to prayer seems gradually to be a cul de sac, blocking you rather than opening up the way, then there are other ways, all of which have been used as approaches in the Bible. So we're not considering anything as a preparation for prayer which hasn't been tried and spoken about in scripture.

Breathing God in

Most of us lead busy lives and have many calls on our time and energy. Perhaps we could spend hours in preparation for being there for God if we really wanted to. After all, Jesus, who was surrounded by and responded to the claims of others all day long, crept away to the hills at night to be with his Father. But, if we're honest, not many of us are going to do that. At the end of a long day, the call of a warm bed drowns out most other calls. So we may only occasionally be able to enter into extended imaginative reading of scripture. However, we breathe every moment that we're alive and our breathing can, itself, help us to be ready for God. Breath was very important to the writers of the Bible, for breath meant life. In a sense, as you breathed, you breathed in God, and Jesus gave his spirit to his disciples through breathing on them. We can still breathe in a way that helps us to be aware of the Lord.

Try this. Stand upright but relaxed with your arms by your sides and your palms facing outwards in receptivity. Look up slightly. Now breathe in slowly and gently. When you are ready, breathe in a way which expresses the thought, "I long for you, Lord." Now breathe in a way which expresses, "I offer myself to you." Don't say the words, breathe them. Ask the Holy Spirit to help you to breathe more of your love for God.

Try this prayer. Don't say the words, breathe them.

> Lord Jesus Christ,
> Son of God,
> Have mercy on me,
> A sinner.

Each of the four lines can be keyed into your breath. You breathe in and as you do so, take in the thought of the first line. Line two is thought whilst breathing out, line three in again and the final line, out. Gradually, your body, your thought and your heart come together in a longing for God.

With the stilling of our inner clamour, our sense of

wonder and worship start to escape from the thousand and
one busynesses and preoccupations with which we enmesh
them. As the prayer is breathed in and out then, perhaps,
our wonder at the mystery of our own bodies surprises us.
The Psalmist ponders this in Psalm 139:2–3:

> Thou knowest all, whether I sit down or rise up;
> Thou hast discerned my thoughts from afar.
> Thou hast traced my journey and my resting places,
> and art familiar with all my paths.

It was as I learned to relate my breathing to my desire for
God that I discovered the Lord is closer to me than I am to
myself. He has already accepted the mystery of all that I
don't understand about myself, and calls me to follow him
there.

Knowing God

The Psalmist goes on to cry out that "Such knowledge is
beyond my understanding". In being there for God as
Jesus was there for God we are seeking a knowledge that
is beyond our understanding. And for a lot of us that's
rather a frightening prospect. We live in a society which
is increasingly dependent on exact understanding. I'm
writing this on a word processor and I'm grateful to the
technology that has made that possible. But despite the
large part it plays in our lives and the chunks of our
energy it consumes, such knowledge isn't the only form of
knowing. What about the knowledge we experience when
we listen to great music – at those times when the chords
of the music set up resonances in our own lives? What
about the knowledge of relationships?

Think now of someone you are close to or have been close
to. If I ask you to describe that person to me, how will you
do it? I asked a friend to describe his wife. He started with,
"She's dark, going a bit grey now, with blue eyes and rosy
cheeks," then moved on to her personality, "She can be
very kind, a bit bad-tempered at times, got a good sense of
humour but doesn't bear fools gladly."

I then prodded. "How d'you know?"

My friend looked startled but came up with, "I've watched her in various situations." The reply was a vague summing up of the film run fast forward through his memory in search of situations when she'd been kind or bad-tempered or when one of her witty replies had rippled a smile round the room.

How has he gained his knowledge of his wife? Through observing her with others and through living with her himself. His knowledge has developed as his relationship has developed. He may at times have been bored by her or disliked her, felt angry with her or wanted to get away from her. But in all these responses, he's still got to know more of her. He has entered further into the mystery of another person. If he stopped relating to her, he might still be able to describe her but his marriage would no longer be part of the foundation of his life.

We can learn once and for all how to switch on the TV and, if we don't bother with it for a year, the knowledge will still be at our fingertips. But could you still say you know your wife if you haven't clapped eyes on her for a year? When I meet friends after a time apart, I think I've remembered them accurately, but then just a few minutes in their presence blows away a lot of that remembered knowledge. Their presence is both so much more and sometimes so much less than I thought it was, and I find myself saying, "Oh yes, of course, they're like that. How could I have forgotten?"

The knowledge which is important to us as people, the knowledge which makes us people, is not a defining or a thinking about (the freezing point of water is 0° C), nor a once and for all know-how, but a continual exploring in relationship. It is the knowledge required through moving out of ourself towards another. God is always moving out of himself in love and we are made in his image. So getting to know a wife is not learning to think about her, nor is it just observing her effect on others. It is the continual, life-long process of receiving and giving in a knowledge that is beyond understanding. It is love. And at times it may be something like hate.

God, being himself the Love from which all our moving out from ourselves in love comes, can only be known through relationship. We cannot know him by thinking about him. He is beyond the understanding of our intellect. We can and do construct creeds and they have their place just as, if my wife goes missing, the ability to describe her in terms of her hair and eye colouring has its uses. Also, it's handy to be able to answer the question, "What's she like?" However, talking about a person or thinking about a person doesn't help us into a knowledge of a person in a way which changes us. She's got dark hair – so what? She's quick witted – what does that matter? But running my fingers through the dark hair, brushing it, feeling its softness, smelling its freshness and experiencing, with a twinge, the passing of the years in its first grey streaks, that's what a marriage is about. That changes me. That's the stuff of joy.

We come to God as people. So our relationship with him must also be beyond thinking and beyond defining. Theologically, we may be able to say that God is love; we may be able to think that God is love. But we feel nothing. Prayer is the process of being discovered by God. We explore God and we are explored by him. Prayer is entering into the experience of love. Where God is concerned, it is love itself which is knowledge, and there is no other way of knowing. That is why all our preparations for prayer have been geared to prompting us not into definition or thought but into response: not into having discussions about the love of God but into some ways of experiencing both wonder and stillness so that we can start to be there for God. We can start to look at and receive his love. Talking and defining have to stop. Thinking must fade. Such prayer is an affair of the heart. It is knowledge beyond understanding. Love alone is its knowing and we enter it in the name of love.

Lord, mould in us a space for your love.

3

OPENING UP

When the speaking stops, when we still our thinking, what sort of language is left? Once you've left behind the chat and activity which can prove so effective in keeping God at bay, you may immediately become aware of God's presence and of his peace. But some people find the silence scary. You may at first feel a little unease or even fear. It may seem as if you're in a sort of no-man's-land between the smokescreen of your old ways and the presence of God which doesn't seem very close as yet. In prayer itself, perhaps you don't feel as if much is happening. God is there. And love is imaginative, love speaks to us in many ways, and you may start to sense new forms of communication which don't necessarily come to you at the times you've set aside for prayer. Let's look first at some of the ways which are more obvious, and so, easier for us to describe to other people . . .

Twenty years ago, when I was studying in York, four of us, all girls, lived in a house together. One morning Jane and I were working in the university library when, suddenly, she looked up from her books and whispered, "I've got to go back to the house."

"Why?"

"Can't say," she looked perplexed.

"Don't be daft," I countered. "You must have some idea."

"No. It's just a very, very strong feeling."

I was about to press her on the point when I noticed a boy at the next table glaring at me to be quiet. I looked down in embarrassment, and by the time I looked up again, Jane had gone.

When I got back to the house at lunchtime, she

explained to me. "It was John." John was a travelling secretary from one of the Christian associations who visited us quite regularly and had just finished one of his trips. "He should have got the train earlier this morning. He was due in Manchester for tomorrow. Anyway, when I got back, he was practically doubled up outside our house, hanging on to the railings."

That sounded dramatic enough. "Where is he now?"

"He's in the General. I got him inside and rang for an ambulance. They whisked him in pretty quick. I went too. It's suspected appendicitis. They're waiting for a consultant to have a look at him. I can ring about four."

It was appendicitis, and John was operated on. He'd been walking to the station when the pain tore through him. He didn't know what to do but wasn't far from our house at the time. When Jane found him clinging to the railings, he was trying to get as far as the door to knock and see if any of us were in.

One summer's day about three years ago, I'd put the morning aside for reading. It was a much looked forward to break. I'd just finished a heavy bout of teaching and felt the need to wind down and relax. A very close, older friend lived in the next road, in fact our gardens butted on to one another. She'd not been too well recently and I'd popped in the previous day to see how she was. I wasn't due to visit her again until the end of the week. I was less than pleased when I couldn't get Mary out of my mind all that morning. Normally my concentration is good and I have no trouble getting totally involved with what I'm reading but that morning my mind flitted and skimmed over the words, sliding from one sentence to the next and touching down nowhere. I was reduced to reading a page three times and still not being sure what was written there. The rest of me joined in the jig of inattention and I found myself prowling from room to room in a state of red alert. Everything in me was reacting as if something was wrong but there was no obvious cause for such concern.

The phone rang. Its interruption was almost a relief.

"Rosemary?" a voice I recognised at once as that of Mary's GP made sure it was me at the end of the line.

"I'll come at once," I responded.

"Where to?" He sounded very surprised.

"To Mary's. You're there, aren't you?" I checked.

"Yes," more surprised.

"D'you want me to take her in immediately?"

"There's no desperate rush but within the hour might be a good idea."

"OK. I'll be with you in about five minutes."

I put the receiver down and hardly had time to notice that the anxiety had drained away completely as I swung into action. Nor was it until the next day that I went over the conversation and realised that I knew Mary needed hospital treatment without being told. No wonder the doctor had sounded a little surprised.

Love's communication

What are we to make of such stories? Do we note that the main participants are women? Should we put it down to the female temperament, that peculiar phenomenon we label anything from hysteria to the sixth sense? Perhaps we're tempted to. But what of churches these days with a healing ministry, both physical and emotional? What of the upsurge in prophecy and of the pictures that so many are now seeing in prayer? What do we make of people who say that God is communicating with them through dreams or visions, and who receive what they call words of knowledge? I read recently of a church in America where some of the leaders clearly "saw" the name of a person's sin written on that person's forehead. How terrible to have the secrets of one's life open to view! That depends on the response of the viewer. There's the Peeping Tom of curiosity or the jubilation of the self-righteous, "There you are. Caught you at it. Always knew you were wicked through and through." Or there's the burning, forgiving love of God whose seeing is an opportunity to extend an invitation to repentance and a new life of abundance. Such seeing is then followed by the addition of new Christians to the Church. Are there any precedents for this?

All these forms of communication are mentioned in scripture as ways in which God related to his people. In Genesis 28:12, we read that Jacob dreamt and saw a ladder stretching up from earth to heaven with angels going up and down it. God interpreted the dream for him as a promise that the land should be his and that both he and his descendants would be blessed and protected and brought back to that land.

Acts 10:9–16 speaks of a vision which changed Peter's life. Isaiah 6:1–7 recounts the magnificent vision of the prophet who saw "the Lord seated on a throne, high and exalted, and the skirt of his robe filled the temple." This is a little different from the vision of Peter in that it is not related to a specific, urgent problem in the world but gives us an indication of the wonder of God. Isaiah's response is the appropriate, "Woe is me! I am lost, for I am a man of unclean lips".

Philip was given strict instructions by an angel to "start out and go south to the road that leads down from Jerusalem to Gaza." (Acts 8:26)

Jesus frequently "knew" those people he was speaking to. "When Jesus saw Nathaniel coming, he said, 'Here is an Israelite worthy of the name; there is nothing false in him.' Nathaniel asked him, 'How do you come to know me?' Jesus replied, 'I saw you under the fig-tree before Philip spoke to you.'" (John 1:47–48) The knowing resulted from Jesus' way of God-like seeing with an intensity and clarity and compassion which penetrate the heart. The more we allow people and things to be themselves for us without trying to manipulate them (and Jesus never manipulated) the more we see clearly. That is why we declare, "God sees us." It is one way of trying to express both the intensity of the concern God has for us and the extent of the freedom he encourages in us. We are to be free as he is free. Such a seeing is contemplation, an appreciation of the person or object in itself with as much love and perception as we are capable of. Jesus contemplated everything and so knew what made people tick. He entered into the mystery of things. There's a curious rule that the further we enter into the mystery of what is, the less it is mystification to us. We read in John 2:24–25, "He knew men so well, all of them, that he needed no evidence from others about a man, for he himself could tell what was in a man." Such insight is not a magic trick, a sort of optional extra to the personality. Jesus' insight was an integral part of the sort of person he was. He "knew" because that was the level on which he related. We need not fear such clarity for it is the clear-sightedness of acceptance and offering. It is a seeing which seeks to lead us to joy.

Whole books in the Bible are devoted to prophecy; that is, to the telling forth in a situation of the will of God for that situation. There may sometimes be indications about the future too. God prophesied through people who were attentive to his heart and Spirit. How else could they have "told forth"? Joel 2:28 holds out the amazing promise, "Thereafter the day shall come when I will pour out my spirit on all mankind: your sons and your daughters shall prophesy, your old men dream dreams, and your young men see visions . . ."

Can such unusual forms of communication be valid now? The validity of anything depends on whether or not it lives as part of the truth of God. Once we understand that the truth of God is the mysterious, unfolding truth of love, we can then ask, what is the language of love?

It's quite usual for people who've lived together for some time to find they are developing the same thoughts. Sympathy below the level of reasoning has woven a web of communication. So her, "How about Devon for our holidays this year?" is met with his, "Funny you should say that, I was thinking of Devon too." Sometimes we see a resemblance between an older man and wife. The likeness isn't one of bone structure or feature, it's the indefinable "something" of shared expressions in a lifetime's moulding of face and gesture independent of words. The deeper the love, the more the entire person is involved in communication. In the Godhead the love is so complete that the Father in his entirety is offered to the Son and the Son in every aspect relates to his Father. The leaping of that relationship is what we call the Spirit of God. In love, deep calls to deep and Spirit communes with Spirit. St. Paul explains that the same is true of the relationship between God and a person. "The Spirit of God joins with our spirit in testifying that we are God's children . . ." (Romans 8:16) The language of love is direct, swift, straight to the centre of the life and the imagination. It is a language which is both a sword piercing the heart and a light sparking connections where before there was only darkness or an inability to express ourselves.

The importance of the non-rational

Under the tutelage of God's Spirit, levels of our personality previously dead to us are coaxed into life. Our imagination starts to speak to us, our capacity for visual image takes on form and colour and the discernment of love helps us to understand intuitively at least a little of what is forming the core of the life of someone else. All this is what scripture calls the gifts of the Spirit. All this is part of the way in which our Father is encouraging us to be whole.

It seems that Jesus found all the levels of his personality accessible to him. To the extent that we are still enough to open our depths to God, to that extent we too become in touch with ourselves. This being in touch enables God's being in touch with us. He is always trying to love us into life and relationship at all levels and in every facet of what we are.

If we insist that we exist only as our rational selves then we are living on the top of a very slippery iceberg. We are most vulnerable then to sliding down into sudden bouts of behaviour or attitude which shock both us and others. We say, "Oh that's just not in character at all!" It certainly is in character to the extent that our unadmitted nine tenths, our unacknowledged depths, have thrown their

weight at us and upended the reasonableness of which we
were so proud.

God never bullies us. He offers us freedom, freedom to be
as much ourselves as we are capable. God, being totally
capable, is both totally himself and totally free. Part of our
growth into freedom is to acknowledge that the super-
rational in ourselves is also open to God. If we don't admit
this then we voluntarily padlock ourselves in behind a
soundproof glass screen and then complain that we can't
sense God communicating with us. There's a picture in the
Tate Gallery which illustrates just this cut-offness. It
shows a figure imprisoned in a glass cage. His clothes are
immaculate and he's sitting correctly upright. But the
mouth is open wide and screaming with an anguish that
burns the clothes to sackcloth and slays the uprightness
into rigor mortis. To the extent that I fail to allow the
Spirit of God to work his powerful integration in me, to
that extent is my uprightness a kind of death. Jesus said to
his followers, "Everything I do, you shall do and more."
(John 14:12) I quail when I read those words for they are a
reproach to me at every level. Because there are depths in
me still inaccessible both to myself and to God, the world
and other people are poorer and I am not glorifying God.
Part of the journey of prayer is to co-operate with the
Spirit who continually encourages me to acknowledge
more of myself and, having acknowledged that, to invite
his wholeness into that area. More and more it seems to
me that the task of being alive is to carve out a capacity for
God.

Testing the spirits

Perhaps we sense that these biblical understandings
through love are valid at least in theory. But how are we to
know when the word of knowledge which someone receives is a word bringing life? Or when the picture described relates to something other than the person's wish
fulfilment? Acknowledgement of the super-rational in us

is not to be confused with a *carte blanche* acceptance of everything it throws at us. We know how devious our conscious mind can be. It's not a question that the conscious mind takes us away from God while the formerly inaccessible necessarily leads us home to God. Jesus was under no illusions about that. He said, "A good man produces good from the store of good within himself; and an evil man from evil within produces evil." (Matthew 12:35) Most of us are a mishmash of good and bad: we can produce breathtaking generosity and then a pincering of malice straight after it in a way which horrifies us. Our rational and super-rational selves can alike both make us more available and less available to God.

So, how are we to know when something we sense is of God really is in accord with his ways? We can use the same tests both for what we have thought out and for what we feel is a message from God through more intuitive means. If I have an idea I can ask:

1) Does it fit in with what I know of the character of God in scripture? This assumes that I give time and attention to the reading and study of scripture.

2) Does it encourage relationships? Is it creative as the love of God is creative or is it a flaunting of *my* ideas, *my* opinions, *my* desires?

3) Is it pompous and out of proportion with the situation to which it addresses itself? In other words, am I taking a sledgehammer to crack a nut?

I can ask myself the identical questions regarding any of what I consider to be gifts of the Spirit, remembering that just because they seem to be more mysterious or vivid or powerful, altogether more "spiritual", this is no proof of their working for good. The devil is vivid, powerful and altogether spiritual – this does not make him a messenger from God!

Using these criteria I've suggested, and you may be able to think of more, let's look at the stories at the beginning of the chapter. Are they the real thing, glinting with relationship and in harmony with God's heart, or are they cheap, dull, paste imitations?

The form of communication is valid in scripture. Jane said, "I've got to go back to the house." Isn't this something of what scripture means when it expresses itself in words like, "The Spirit said to him", or "these two sent out on their mission by the Holy Spirit"? Neither Jane nor I felt the sense of command to do something against an instruction laid down in scripture, or at a time when others would have been inconvenienced or hurt by us following "the urge". So the morality of the biblical God is not infringed. In both cases relationship was encouraged in that someone needed help and God provided a trusted friend. Again, in both cases, the situation only swung into focus camera-shot by camera-shot. The Israelites were given food by God every day in the wilderness and were told only to collect one day's allowance at a time. In the same way, as the first part of the command was followed, the next part became clearer. We live by faith not by sight, and the key to such living is an obedience rooted in humility.

Who's talking?

Now let's look at another two situations which I know have arisen in the last couple of years. In the first, a woman who had been part of a small Christian group meeting once a week for over a year within the church became increasingly uneasy both with the leadership of the group and with her position in it. She was the leader of another small group meeting regularly and appeared to be at ease with her own leadership. Finally, she left the group but returned once or twice, as she explained, "just to visit". On her third visit she told the group she had a word from the Lord and that God had instructed her to tell the remaining members that they needed to love each other more. The group prayed in response to her statement, prayer which was interrupted by a further accusation that someone present wasn't really believing.

The second incident concerns a couple whom a church's

leadership has recognised have a particular ministry of prayer. People with problems are sent to the couple. Recently, a woman whose marriage has been rocky was asked to visit them. When she arrived they welcomed her and shared with her what the Lord had revealed to them about her situation. "But it's not like that at all," she explained. Some of the "facts" they recounted she felt were far from accurate. She felt entirely unable to disagree with them further when they replied, "But, my dear, we have what we've told you from the Lord."

If we look at the first occasion I mentioned, none of us could quarrel with the message that the former group member gave. It's unlikely that whatever situation we're in, we love each other enough. But what is more troubling is her own position in relation to the group when she gave her "word". It's this that we may sense doesn't quite fit in with the God of scripture. In God there is complete integration. He loves because he is love and he judges because he is just. His freedom lies in this integration. What he does, he is. So he never ducks the responsibility for his actions. When he wants to love his creation, he demonstrates that love. He doesn't just exhort us to love, he becomes part of the created world and loves within it. In short, he takes on personhood. He expresses himself in Jesus. It is not in the character of God to goad the team on from the sidelines, especially if what he says is not going to make him popular. Our words, or "word", are only valid to the extent that we are prepared to live out the responsibility for them. The former group member had made sure that she was well out of any responsibility before delivering her exhortation. So is she in line with the character of God? What about relationship? If she is encouraging relationship, then she isn't prepared to take part in the painful creativity of building more love. How does this compare with Jesus, the Servant King?

In the second incident the praying couple have a choice to make. Do they choose relationship and listen to the woman whose life they have become involved in? Or do they choose the opposite of relationship, discount what another person is trying to communicate and follow their individualism? They seem to have opted for the latter. Because God is love, the Father always moving out of himself towards the Son and the Son responding in the dance that created the universe, any retreat away from relationship and into individualism in a situation is a retreat from God in that situation.

We may use the word "God", we may speak of "messages from the Lord" but we must test such knowing. Understanding given by God is rooted in humility. Humility flourishes in relationship and it brings forth the fruit of common or garden, down-to-earth humanity, which includes compassion, an ability to listen to one another and taking responsibility for our actions. Humility is essentially creative and involved as God is creative and involved.

God's language is love but I sometimes wonder how loving my use of his name is at times. If I'm speaking with a brother or sister and I say, "The Lord has given me this idea", or "The Lord has told me to tell you . . .", how much am I respecting the freedom of others? How much am I encouraging relationship? What of growth and creativity? Despite the use of the Name, aren't I rather blocking others? If they wish to disagree with me, can they? Doesn't it seem as if they're going against the Lord? Am I so afraid to trust others that I can't speak plainly and suggest, "How about?" or "What if?" In response to Jesus' plea for simple language, I'd like to learn to speak in such a way that other people are encouraged to be more themselves both by my words and by my listening. But I'm a long way from that. My laziness and individualism get in the way.

Aspects of love

Jesus was well aware of how often we debase the coinage of our relationship with him by the inclusion of the lead filings of our individualism. He gives terrifying teaching in which gifts more powerful than language are concerned. We can find this teaching in Matthew 7:21–23. It's

blood-chilling in its condemnation of our tendency to think
that the spiritual powers which become available to us
at levels beyond the rational, are more important than
relationships. "When the day comes, many will say to me,
'Lord, Lord, did we not prophesy in your name, cast out
devils in your name, and in your name perform many
miracles?' Then I will tell them to their face, 'I never knew
you; out of my sight, you and your wicked ways!'" Again,
in Matthew 25:31–46 we read that at judgment we are to
be separated into sheep who will be led to possess the
kingdom and goats who are to be cursed and banished
from the presence of God. Why this division, and why the
rejection? Because some came across people in distress,
the hungry and thirsty and those in prison and had helped
them. They didn't feel religious about it and when Jesus
says they did these things for him, they question, "Lord,
when was it that we saw you hungry and fed you, or thirsty
and gave you a drink?" The reply comes, "I tell you this:
anything that you did for one of my brothers here, however
humble, you did for me." The reverse is true for the goats
who didn't relate with compassion. They failed to recognise the connections in the universe. Jesus tells them,
"Anything you did not do for one of these, however
humble, you did not do for me."

There doesn't seem so much to be a horizontal axis to our
lives which we call our earthly relationships and a vertical
axis which we call our relationship with God. Rather,
both are aspects of the same thing. Our elder daughter,
Catherine, often twists her hair into the intricacies of a
french plait. The completed plait is the result of the
threading together of diverse strands of hair. Take a
strand out and there's no plait: try to say which strand is
more important to the plait as a whole and you can't. To
me, our relationships with God and with people are like
that: it's not advisable to try to unravel the strands if you
want to keep together a completed life. That is why Jesus
says that the touchstone of our love for him is our
relationship with other people. God, whom we can't
see, will judge the quality of our devotion to him by

how much we have been prepared to love what we can see.

All this is enough to make those of us convinced of the validity of right prophesying and the correct use of the intuitive powers decide to give up on it all. But that would be to throw out the baby with the bath water. God does not make the exercise of spiritual gifts an opposition to caring relationships; it is we alone who can do that if we use gifts for the wrong reasons, perhaps as a reinforcement of our power rather than as service to others. The gifts of the Spirit and the fruit of the Spirit are alike given to increase the depth of our relationships and to glorify God in his creation as a whole.

We can take encouragement from Jesus' teaching to his followers when they return to him jubilant having exercised the gifts of the Spirit. They found out that, "In your name, Lord . . . even the devils submit to us." (Luke 10:17) Gently he encourages their first steps in the realms of principalities and powers, "And now you see that I have given you the power . . . and nothing will ever harm you." But then, as a good shepherd guides overexcited and self-orientated sheep back from the track of individualism and on to the path of love, he reminds them, "Nevertheless, what you should rejoice over is not that the spirits submit to you, but that your names are enrolled in heaven." Heaven is not only an after-death word, it is a word which describes the fullness of life in God here and now, that is, the fullness of creative love.

So powers other than the rational are to be encouraged but their life is to be sifted and tested in humility by the criterion of our knowledge of the God of scripture. Above all, we are never to mistake the fruits of a deepening relationship with God for the root of that relationship itself. This root is the love which forms and connects the universe, the love in which we "live and move . . . [and] exist." (Acts 17:28) It's rather like a marriage. From time to time the abiding quality of the relationship between a husband and wife will result in creativity for others; on a very simple physical level their making love may result in

the new life of children. But the children are the products
of the love – everyone's got problems if they confuse the
children with the love itself. Children come and children
go but the marriage continues.

The children are what we can see of the creative love of a
marriage. Sometimes the gifts of the Spirit are what we
can see of the deepening relationship between God and his
people. We often seem to be tempted to walk by sight, to tot
up the evidence rather than to follow in the darkness of
faith. We choose a knowing about rather than an exploration in relationship with all the patience and care that
takes. We want to put our finger on things and proclaim,
"This is it!" This is all too soon followed by, "Got it!" This is
just how the disciples were, thrilled to bits with proclaiming, "Got it!" Jesus didn't let them get away with it. The
early Christians at Corinth succumbed to the same temptation and flaunted their spiritual gifts in an "I'm holier
than thou" fashion which caused factions and later the
fracture of individual judgment. Faction and fracture can
still erupt especially over what many people today call
prophecy. Biblical prophecy is the telling forth of God who
is Lord of all men, interested in the connection of relationship above the flaunting of spectacular powers. We
show off spiritual powers because deep within us lies the
tendency to try to possess our experiences, to cry out, "Got
it!" "Got it!" always causes schism because "Got it!" means
I possess it, and, if I possess it, I have to defend it. Also, if I
possess it, you can't, can you? I must be right and you must
be wrong, for we all know that possession is nine-tenths of
the law. So I have cleaved a great divide between you and
me by using the gifts of the Spirit against the Spirit
himself. I have tarnished the image of love which the
Creator has imprinted in me. The test of our submission to
Jesus is our willingness to submit to each other. We follow
a Servant King. So, the marks of a prophecy from God are
frequently to do with repentance, that call to turn, turn,
turn ourselves to God in every aspect of our lives. The
biblical prophets speak of our responsibilities to each
other within society. Like Jesus, they pour scathing anger

on a religion which tries to ignore relationships, for such a
religion is not known by God. It is idolatry.

Very early on in the life of the Church someone saw the
power of God operating and, like I so often do, hoped he
could separate the fruits of this power from its root of
relating love. On the generally accepted principle that,
"everything has its price" Simon, a magician, already
quite proficient in his art and so bowled over by Christian
teaching and the "signs" following that he'd been bap-
tised, approached Peter, offered him money and begged,
"Give me the same power too, so that when I lay hands on
anyone, he will receive the Holy Spirit." (Acts 8:19–20)
Before we leap to condemn such a request, let's ask
ourselves how we respond to free grace? Isn't it scary, all
that generosity and my own self-evaluation irrelevant? So
much neater to quantify and pay for and possess. There we
have it again, the "Got it!" outlook.

It's not surprising that the man who hoped to buy the
Holy Spirit was a magician. Magic is manipulative power
and its attraction lies deep in all of us. One day at the end
of last year, Susannah and I were walking through the
park at the back of our house. It was late afternoon, the
time when a purpling haze plays tricks with distance and
perspective. The central avenue of trees bisecting the
gardens had already lost their leaves and skeletal
branches brushed the sky with a rustle of bony fingers.
Suddenly, Susannah jerked away from me. "I'm going to
catch the wind," she declared and whooped as she ran in
imitation of its gusts and bursts. I watched while she
skipped up and down the path. One of the wind's tails
flipped her scarf across her eyes. She pulled it back with a
laugh and a "tut". The wind galloped in her hair this way
and that, riding it, tearing at its roots, hard and demanding. A lighter touch sent the hem of her coat into ripples.
Her cheeks grew pink as she ran, finally dodging behind
the fat bole of one of the older limes. I found her there,
leaning back against the bark, eyes closed and breathless.

"Well, where is it?" I asked.

She opened one eye to peer at me, "Where's what?"

"The wind. You did catch it, didn't you?"

She shut the eye again. "Let's go home," she suggested by way of a change of subject.

So we did.

Susannah had not caught the wind but the wind in an amazing variety of speeds and touches had caught her – hair, eyes, cheeks, legs, energy. It had caught her, bowled through her and showed not the slightest dent in its energy for having done so. But Susannah was left with the imprint of the encounter. As Jesus said, "The wind blows where it wills; you hear the sound of it, but you do not know where it comes from, or where it is going." (John 3:8)

The breath of the Spirit blows where he wills. We can only put ourselves in his path and respond when he wants to communicate.

Forgive me, Lord when I try to hold your Spirit
Teach me, Jesus, to turn my face to the breath of your
   Spirit
Blow on me, wind of God: give me wonder at your
   power and gentleness.

4

TRAVELLING TOGETHER

Henry is the son of a friend of mine. Henry is three, and when he's cross, which is quite often at the moment, he runs squealing through my friend's house. He puts the sitting room with its fitted carpet and the hall, landing and stairs with their fitted carpets behind him. He's heading for the spare bedroom. Money for fitted carpets ran out there and bare boards surround the large rug which covers much of the floor. Henry loves the bare boards. He rushes straight to the largest exposed area of wood near the bay window and, once there, stamps in fury. The pistol shot claps of hard shoes on hard board resound satisfyingly clearly throughout the house. Henry is asserting his independence. Once the storm's over, he's equally demanding of a cuddle from his mother. Then he's asserting his desire to belong.

A year or so back there was a slogan for cream cakes which ran, "naughty but nice". It was amazingly success-ful – not surprisingly, for it appealed to the Henry in all of us, whatever our ages. "Naughty" which stamps, "Ya boo, I'm me and I don't have to be like you." And "Nice" which says, "But I'm really awfully good for all that, and you do love me, don't you?"

We all long to love and be loved, and in that way we show the marks of God's image burned in us. But we all fear being consumed, "eaten up" by a relationship until we no longer exist. In that sense too, we show the marks of God's image burned in us. For the Father, Son and con-necting Spirit love each other totally and, at the same time, they are totally free. They give everything but they remain distinct. Distinction is necessary for relationships; as the old saying goes, "It takes two to tango."

As we become more open to God, so our capacity for relationship flexes and grows. I understand increasingly that I am only fully me in relationship and, at the same time, that I will not be swallowed up by any giving. It is as Jesus said, "A man's life does not consist in the abundance of his possessions." (Luke 12:15, New International Version) In one of those strange balances of life, as we allow others to be more themselves, not dominating or possessing them, and as we allow God to be more himself, so we become more aware that we are all connected together. We feel less alone.

The Holy Spirit

Perhaps one of our first steps out from ourselves is the understanding that it is God's Spirit who has called us to pray. We are never alone. It is the Holy Spirit who gives us the invitation to "Come", and the Spirit who woos and encourages us. We make the first marvellous discovery that it is not so much me trying to get through to God but that it is God who is always yearning to bring me to himself. Our spiritual life flourishes not when we realise that we love God but when we start to take in some of the enormity of the love that God has for us.

The company of Heaven

No prayer is private. Whenever we pray, we are joining the eternal celebration of all God's people, living and dead and to come. Some of the saints have been very aware of the love which surrounds them. When Saint Catherine of Genoa was on her death bed, her tired face suddenly lit up with delight.

One of her friends by the bedside asked her, "What is it?"

"I see so many happy faces," she replied.

Another dying Christian suddenly exclaimed, "Oh, I see I am so loved!" She, too, had glimpsed something of what is real but usually unseen.

Our praying is a gateway into reality. All that means is that Heaven is a celebration. When we pray, we enter, among other things, the love, joy and delight of those who already see God face to face. As the Church of England modern service of the eucharist puts it, "With angels and archangels, and with all the company of heaven, we proclaim your great and glorious name, for ever praising you . . ."

Graham Greene at the end of *Monsignor Quixote* puts it another way. Father Quixote, a gentle and, just before he died, confused priest, is mourned by his friend the communist ex-mayor of El Toboso. The ex-mayor muses, "Why is it that the hate of man – even of a man like Franco – dies with his death, and yet love . . . seemed now to live and grow in spite of the final separation and the final silence – and for how long, he wondered with a kind of fear, was it possible for that love of his to continue? And to what end?"

Is it possible for that love to grow out of all proportion to the seeds of love we experience now, just as Jesus explained that a huge mustard tree starts out as a tiny seed rolling in the palm of one human hand? And is it possible for this love to continue? Oh yes, for it is the only thing about us that will continue. Ultimately, God can only recognise himself. He is love and we are only alive in so far as we live in love. And to what end? That we learn to take our first, hesitant, two left-footed steps in the eternal dance of celebration which is the life of God and the company of Heaven.

Jesus and the citizens of Heaven are as real as the room you're sitting in, as real as the people around you. Not being restricted by physical boundaries, they are closer than either. They are, incidentally, more in touch with you than you are with yourself. Our prayer is a lifetime's exploration but God is everywhere, we discover, before we are, both in our inward and our outer growth.

Jesus and the company of Heaven enjoy us. God looks at us with pleasure. We may feel we're not very attractive. Perhaps the baby's been sick over your clothes or you're losing the energy of youth. Perhaps you're overweight or

weary of squandered relationships and unfulfilled possibilities. But God looks at us with an acceptance and a
passion that make nonsense of our self-distaste.

As we dare to return his gaze, first luxuriating in his
love and then looking at him, so we learn to enjoy the
society of his friends. Can we suspect that, like Jesus, they
retain their interest in us after death? One of them, Teresa
Martin, was quite clear that she wasn't going to give up her
love of people on earth when she was dead. She announced
very firmly, "I shall spend my Heaven doing good on
earth." The community of saints still stretch out hands to
us across the silence.

Angels

With me no longer alone at the centre of it, my world grows
larger. I can start to enjoy the relationships of a much
richer and more diverse universe. Perhaps I've felt there
was only God and me or, at best, God and other people. But
now there's an invitation to become part of a rather larger,
vastly more satisfying society. There are the "witnesses to
faith around us like a cloud" (Hebrews 12:1): angels,
archangels, cherubim and seraphim and the unnamed
inhabitants of the seven heavens that St. Paul speaks of.
What a richness of relationship! And one which we are
tempted to neglect. An encouragement to live in a reality
which includes angels came to me through a cartoon.
Sometimes the Holy Spirit seems the master of the one
line throw-away.

The cartoon showed a hearty woman dressed in tweeds
sitting at the wheel of her ancient car. It was clear she was
about to set off for a drive with her companion, a smaller,
more timid person, in tow. The expression on the companion's face was one of such alarm that even the insensitive driver picked it up. "Don't worry," she assured her, "I
always just say a quick prayer to my guardian angel, and
everything's all right." As my eyes travelled down to the
bottom of the picture, they caught sight of a very squashed
guardian angel pinned under the car wheels. His head

stuck out under one side of the vehicle, a look of resigna-
tion so deep all over his face that it seemed it had become a
permanent expression. Obviously, this was not his first
experience of her driving!

In the Bible we read of angels as messengers of God – it
was the Archangel Gabriel who spoke with Mary about
the conception of Jesus, and as the battle force of God.
When God drove Adam and Eve out of the Garden, we
read, "He stationed the cherubim with a sword whirling
and flashing to guard the way to the tree of life." (Genesis
3:24) Angels are the constant go-betweens in different
aspects of reality, reassuring and encouraging, as well as
defending. It was an angel who helped Hagar when she
was alone in the desert, and angels who ministered to
Jesus at the end of his fast. Gabriel interpreted a vision for
Daniel and an angel encouraged St. Paul when his ship
struck difficulties en route for Crete. Scripture is peppered
with the appearances or stories of angels. Perhaps some of
the messengers are seen only with the inner eye in a vision
or dream. There is even the suggestion that we may not be
able to recognise them as such at all; we may, in fact,
"entertain angels unawares."

May we not also be protected by angels without realising it? Think back on your life and ask the Holy Spirit to
help you to pinpoint any incidents where you had no
"right" to come through unscathed, quite the reverse, but
you did. Once you've identified an incident, give thanks for
your safety.

One day last winter, my husband David arrived home
very shocked and upset. Over a cup of tea, he managed to
unravel enough to tell me what had happened. He'd been
driving home as usual from the school where he teaches
when, on the outskirts of one of the villages at a spot where
there's no pavement and where houses open directly on to
the street, a child of about eight years old ran out of her
house, saw his car, misjudged the distance and continued
to run into the road. David glanced to his left; a couple of
women were chatting on the pavement which ran on that
side of the road only. He said he didn't know how he

managed to miss both the women and the child when he careered on to the pavement to avoid the little girl.

Now, if we interpret that as the protection of all concerned by unseen guardians, we are left with the knotty problem of accidents which are not avoided and where people are killed. Perhaps we can only say that God holds all our lives in his hand and that alike, he holds all our deaths. Possibly angels are a means of interpreting and, at times, guarding our lives before the time of our death. Likewise, may they not continue to guard and guide us once our lives have ripened into death? An old Russian proverb states that "Death does not take the old but the ripe." It would seem odd that God's messengers who are at home in many aspects of the creation should abandon us when we move from one form of life in God to another.

Prayer takes the individual and loves the individual into a larger society. When we quieten down enough to "be" in prayer, to sit still and allow God to love us, we find there are others loving us too; angels, archangels and the Christian dead. All these, like God, are on our side. They want to lead us to joy. They want us to start living the abundant life of their presence. They cast off their "pie in the sky when you die" reputation and become part of our here and now. Then we can begin to make friends of them.

Learning to welcome

A taste of any sort of deepening relationship sends us out into deeper relationships with other aspects of our here and now. You can't open up more to God and not open up more to other people. It's just not on the cards. It is God in whom we live, and all aspects of our lives are held in him. For some who are naturally introverted and thin-skinned this isn't easy. But our capacity for welcoming others can be carved out just as we carve out a capacity for God.

A friend, who is now one of the most easy-going and relaxed of people, said that when he was much younger he hated unexpected callers. He was at university doing postgraduate work so it was quite easy for him to hide away with his books all day. He was a Christian and had recently started the prayer of stillness before God. Gradually, he started to realise that he could no longer hang on to his outlook of, "You live your life and I'll live mine. I'm just not the sociable type." At first, when someone knocked on his door he made a conscious prayer before answering, "Thank you God for sending this person. Help me to see you as we meet." Still reluctant, still rather awkward, he opened his door. As he continued his short periods of silence before the Lord, so he absorbed more of the character of God. The image of love began to burn in him, and more and more, people dropped by to chat things over. Love is always attractive. It wasn't until about a year of this had gone by that he realised he no longer consciously prayed as he answered the door. His capacity for relating had grown so that, now spontaneously, he saw God in other people, and spontaneously he welcomed the Lord in every meeting. Generosity had crept up and surprised him when he least expected it. He had found that in prayer we can give ourselves space for the unexpected.

Groups for silent prayer

In my work I often rub shoulders with professional people. They are as different from my shy university friend as chalk from cheese. They live lives in the fast lane, travelling from Europe to the USA or South America, perhaps touching down in the near East or, increasingly now, in Africa as well. Their jobs are demanding and some of them are on the continual red alert of response. But that response doesn't always include an enjoyment of long-term relationships. One of them told me he'd only been home in Spain for a couple of nights in eight weeks. Photos they carry of their children are out of date by the time they return to them. An Austrian said that he no longer had friendships. A series of short-term, stimulating business acquaintanceships had taken their place – all very exciting at first. Unfortunately, like the froth on the top of a cup of coffee, attractive and full of promise, but, once tasted, an insubstantial, melt away to nothing bubble.

So, it isn't just the introverted who find it difficult at first to respond to the call to "Go out from yourself": it's the over-busy, and this includes those who like to keep over-busy because they fear a terrible void in stillness.

Joining a group which meets for silent prayer can help to lead us out from ourselves. The company of others is also a good safety net if you are afraid to entrust yourself to God in silence when you are alone. The structure for such groups can be kept extremely simple. In fact, it's often better that way, then the shy aren't put off by feeling forced to contribute to any introduction, nor does the silence have its power nibbled into by coffee and chat.

For a while, just such a group operated in the church we went to when we lived in Gloucestershire. We met at 9.30 a.m. on a Saturday in one of the side chapels of the building. A member of the group started us off with a short reading – always a good harness for thoughts and emotions if I was having trouble in easing into quiet. I might use meditation on the reading in a slow, systematic pondering of the whole passage, or the mulling over of a word or phrase as a lassoo to guide my energy into the way of quiet. Then breathing the Jesus prayer started to unify mind, imagination and heart. After this, resting in God could take over. The person who read at the beginning closed the meeting promptly at 10 a.m. when he or she led us in saying the Grace together. Then, without chat, we left. That was it; a bare half hour spent together at the start of busy weekends. But, as a result of it, a funny thing happened. We didn't know each other very well and we spanned ages from early twenties to mid eighties but at worship on Sunday we grew aware of bonds forged in the silence. The singing of God's praises together became the outward seal of the silent love of God shared without words. We felt very close to each other within the fellowship of the church. Words which come out of silence and which are enclosed by silence once they've been spoken certainly seem to have a cutting edge about them.

Perhaps that is why the Word which we call Jesus, forged in the silence of eternity, cleaves hearts.

In Canterbury where we live now, a well-established group meets once a month for silence. Its members come from a variety of churches and some from quite a way out of the city. This means that what they experience in the silence cannot be related directly to any one church. The connections are not quite so obvious as they were in Gloucestershire. Because the group meets relatively infrequently it takes a whole evening in which to prepare for silence, keep silence and then say Compline together both as a seal of unity and a link with the prayer of the church as a whole. First there's a quick coffee and then a speaker or a sharing of experiences by the members of the group. In September people talked about how God had spoken to them during the summer break. In a couple of months, a member will share her experience of prayer during illness. Speakers have led meditations on passages of the Bible or have taken the group through an imaginative reading of a gospel story. So, the "lead in" is quite varied. We have used music and listened together or people have brought pictures and photographs which speak to them of God. Those of us who would naturally use one way of preparing ourselves to be still before the Lord have been introduced to a variety of ways. The Church is a body, and prayer, like every aspect of church life, benefits greatly from the arm learning to value the big toe while the hand realises it depends on the foot to keep it above ground.

When we come to silence, we turn the centre lights off and someone puts a match to a candle in the middle of the circle. The flickering but persistent flame acts as a focus for those who respond to symbol. Those who don't can use their own focus. At the end of half an hour's silence, the group sings a hymn and says Compline together.

Another group has just started up and, little by little this is attracting people who are new to the prayer of being still before God. For some, when they first start, half an hour is very demanding. It certainly was for me. I found five minutes dragging on some days and at the end of that time gave in to thinking again with great relief. To respond to differing needs, the group splits into two for prayer. There's half an hour of unbroken silence for those who want it and an option of led meditation with five or so minute periods of silence for those who prefer a "little and often" form of input.

"Dear Diary"

Our going out from ourselves can take different forms. Two of them which are at opposite ends of the spectrum are:

1) Our growing awareness of all sorts of connections where we saw none before.
2) The nagging interruption of distractions when we pray.

We'd probably like to make the most of 1) and silence the chunnerings of 2). For both of these tasks a pencil and note pad or two note pads can come in handy as companions along the way. Let's start with number 2) first.

Sometimes I've prepared for prayer and that's been fine; then I settle down for silence. Any attempt to settle acts as a signal for the yappings of an entire pack of preoccupations and anxieties, like the frenzied barking of a small dog, shredding first the heels and then the entire body of the silence. When this first happened I tried to run for cover back into the safety of meditation or an imaginative exercise. But the second I emerged, there they'd go again: stupid concerns which I could deal with another time – have I posted the gas bill? Do we need more potatoes today or tomorrow? What about that article I said I'd fish out for a student? Small but persistent and destructive. I've found that jotting down preoccupations in a notebook to be referred to at the end of the time of prayer does a lot to silence their whines.

There's a different sort of distraction. What about the blackbird singing on the fence, or the rumble of a lorry down the road? These can be turned into short prayers and then allowed to pass. "Thank you, Lord for the clarity of the birdsong". Then let it go. "Father, I bring before you that lorry driver." The noise is taken into your silence.

The more I have on my plate in an intellectual or harrying sense, the more I need to prepare for prayer, to carve out the capacity for waiting on God for his pleasure. When it's extra difficult to still heart and mind then I suspect my life may be temporarily on overdrive. Sometimes when I'm having enormous difficulties allowing God's silence to rise in me, I'm tempted to give up. But I know from past experience that if I keep at it, turning and turning and turning whatever noise or distraction or niggle which is unsettling me to God, then eventually enough of the superficiality will be scraped away to allow the silence to escape. Maybe not this session, but next session. If I don't keep at it, but give up, then both inclination and capacity are dented. It's like that first, disastrous peep into the biscuit tin if you're trying to diet. But, if you hold out against temptation, then it's that much easier to resist next time.

There's another sort of distraction which can crop up such as persistent memory which reoccurs like a dream whenever we go into quiet. This is not always something which should be silenced. Maybe it's a signal from part of our personality which is not yet accessible to us. Perhaps it's trying to tell us that the telegraph in that area has a longer, as yet undelivered message. In that case, the memory needs to be played back and the event gone through step by step under the guidance of the Holy Spirit. We may even need to take the matter to a counsellor or someone else who can help. Many persistent memories concern hurt or resentment which is so deep that it has not yet been touched by the sifting life of God. While we try to dodge God's touch, the area will retain its poison and, like a running sore, infect more of our life than we are perhaps aware. So what we first interpret as distractions to be jotted down in notebook 2 may fit with greater ease into the realm of connections in notebook 1. Maybe we discover

connections in relationships which are frayed and tattered. In prayer, we become aware of the need for care
and attention or for the so simple but very demanding,
"Sorry". I'd like to consider healing that takes place as we
sit before God in a later chapter.

There are other sorts of connections we can note.
Perhaps in the silence, or as a result of the silence, we
learn to sift our moods more.

When I was fourteen my mother took me to see the film
Ben Hur. I was amazed by it – the spectacle of ancient
Rome, the excitement of the chariot race (all that blood
and guts and, for once, the humans coming off worse than
the horses) and the wonderful detail of costume and set.
Last year the film was shown on TV. Full of expectation, I
switched on. Despite the years, the production techniques
hadn't dated too much, the costumes were as detailed as
ever, some of the photography as haunting, and there was
nothing wrong with the pace of the story. But, slowly at
first and then with a growing confidence, a gloom settled
over me like a fog, blanketing my vitality and seeping into
the pores of my imagination. It wasn't a depression, just a
lowering of spirits.

After a couple of hours I turned the TV off and realised
what the trouble was. The film, demanding nothing of me
except that I get lost in its story, had emptied me out, not
in the positive sense that preparation for prayer can, but
in a way which left me limp and less alive. I'd not been
required to make any effort to relate truly to the film. I'd
just sat back and been smothered by it. So when it was no
longer there, neither was my energy nor any alertness of
spirit. I had unfortunately practised the opposite of Jesus'
advice to "stay awake". My spirit had allowed itself to be
lulled to sleep and the intuitive elements were on shut
down. I felt totally unaware of the presence of God and, in
any case, quite unable to respond to presence of any depth.
I was out of touch with what was real, and felt horribly
alone. Because I realised I'd ushered in the experience
voluntarily, I also felt very sad.

But everything we experience is the voice of God calling

us. Later, in silence before God, I worked to pinpoint what had happened and how I felt. I realised that now, surrendering my inner alertness to something which although fine in itself, for me does nothing except damp the Spirit's life in me. Such surrender does nothing to foster my understanding of the interconnectedness of everything. I'm left feeling cold and alone again.

Reflecting on this, I'm reminded of a story Michael Caine told on TV a little while ago. He was speaking about what he had learned of acting. As a student, he was in a production with a small part only, the equivalent of second spear. He spent most of his time on stage saying nothing. During these long, boring minutes, he switched off.

"What are you doing?" the director called to him.

"Nothing," he replied.

"Oh yes you are," the director said. "You're listening to everything the other people are saying, and you're thinking out replies, only you're not actually speaking the answers."

Michael Caine commented that hearing that completely changed his acting. For the first time he understood that what was required was an inner alertness, a sense of inwardly standing with the weight forward, poised for action even when stationary. In other words, his stillness and silence were not to be heavy and leaden but alert and balanced, prepared for movement.

I find I'm more prepared to respond to the presence of God if my spirit is alert and poised, ready – rather than empty and dull, heavy with non-attention and smothered by an unhelpful surrender to something in the world irrespective of the image of God in it.

Jesus told us a story about this too. We can find it in Matthew 22:1–14. A king prepared a feast for his son's wedding but the invited guests decided at the last minute not to turn up. The king sent his servants out to collect some passers-by from the streets. Good or bad, it didn't matter what they were like. They hadn't known they were going to be dragged in to a wedding and one of them wasn't wearing the right sort of clothes (hardly surprising, we

might think!). Nevertheless, when the king spotted him,
not dressed up, he ordered his servants to tie him up so
that he was helpless and then to turn him out into a
terrible place of wailing and the grinding of teeth. It all
seems horribly unfair. But isn't Jesus trying to tell us that
we should always be prepared for the joy of God? Isn't he
trying to warn us against just the emptiness I felt when I
let my spirit go to sleep? If so, then the seemingly difficult
story contains a teaching of great kindness, for Jesus is
concerned that we should live in the abundance of connect-
ing love. He is seeking to save us from the isolation
brought on by a torpor of spirit which takes us over when
we surrender our attentiveness.

Sifting our moods is part of what St. Paul calls discernment. As we learn discernment so we can begin to choose
for ourselves what most encourages the life of God to stir
in us. We can also learn not to surrender our alertness to
what takes us from God, however good that thing may be
in itself. As St. Paul questions, "'We are free to do anything,' you say. Yes but is everything good for us?" (1
Corinthians 10:23). Our experience of what encourages
our journey to God and what holds out only a cul de sac will
move and change as we move and grow. What wasn't OK
may become perfectly OK and what's OK for some of us,
isn't for others.

I remember a Franciscan friar I knew who was more at
ease and often more charmingly appreciative of the company of women than most men I have come across. He was
neither domineering nor manipulative, and he was quite
ready with a compliment. At first I wondered, was this
flirtation? But flirtation conceals a sharp edge which lends
it an occasional cut and thrust. This Franciscan's charm
was innocent of that. Gradually I came to realise his ease
grew from his rock-solid chastity. He had dedicated all his
love with its sexual energy to God: he had made a promise
to surrender possessive relationships in order to be freer
for all, and as he explained to me once, it wasn't he who
looked after his promise. It was in much safer hands than
his. Jesus held the promise in his hands.

Now, for many of us his ease and charm wouldn't be OK. Our sexuality isn't yet rooted sufficiently in the love of God for us to trust our appreciation of the opposite sex to be pure; that is, to be a genuine appreciation without any desire to cream off a little come-back for ourselves.

As we sift our moods and experience connections we can jot them down in a notebook. If we look back over the notes of several months, often we can trace a pattern which gives us insights into what have been our hidden lives or unknown responses. These insights help us to open our lives up more fully to God and to the leading of his Spirit.

Other mood connections I chart are those relating to sin. Often if I've behaved unlovingly towards someone, or gone in for one-upmanship, showing off, name dropping or plain down-to-earth lack of forgiveness or criticism, I can excuse myself with my mind. Or, failing that, at least damp down the jangle of alarm bells from my conscience. But once I try to settle in stillness before God such unconfessed wrongs or inflicted hurts, anything I can't forgive in another, thunder through the silence deafening any other voice. So again, connections, or the lack of them, are heard. I note them – the next move is the great leap which I don't always take – act to restore harmony, and the Spirit settles once more.

One of the greatest spin-offs of keeping prayer notebooks is that in low times you can remind yourself of the great mercies of God. Also, when you're tempted to give up, you have a record of God's working in your prayer. It's also helpful to use the notebooks to remember in the Bible's use of that word. God told his people to remember their exodus from Egypt, and Jesus told his disciples to break bread and drink wine in remembrance of him. What we often mean by remembering is calling to mind. We think again about an event. What did Jesus mean by remembering? His understanding is much more than that. Biblical remembering is an exercise in drawing the threads of the past through the eye of the needle of the present. Biblical remembering is a reliving: it is to make what was past into a present event. It is not to do with the mind and with thinking. It is to do with the heart and with experiencing. Sometimes I try to remember some of the ways God has been gracious to me in the past. I recall the circumstances of the event or insight. Where was I? Was anyone with me? What was I doing? How did I feel? Was I hot, hungry, happy? Then, what happened? How did the Lord come? How did this increase my understanding and my love? At the end of such a remembering I am reliving my responses and am able to give thanks once more. Present heaviness is transformed into present gratitude by the re-experiencing of past grace, grace which I re-read in my prayer diary.

During a recent bout of crippling temptation, it was a great help to look up similar periods in my notebook and to understand that I had "sat through" seemingly over-whelming compulsions before. Now, when I again want something or am longing to say something best left un-said, I know that if I sit tight the desire will pass. Irri-tations flare and will die just as they have in the past if I have not fed them. My prayer notebook also records that such sitting through is not easy at first. It has on occasions produced sweat and a knotted stomach.

My prayer diary has been a kind of friend. Perhaps such a feeling is common, which is why people have often begun entries with "Dear Diary". The more sense of friendliness we can develop around us, the more encouraged we are to experience that it is love which makes the world go round. In fact we need in prayer, not to think much, but to be as loving as we can.

Spiritual guides

Friendship of a special kind has often featured in the foreground of journeys towards God. I am talking about the friendship of someone whose advice on spiritual mat-ters we can trust. The journey both to connect with ourselves and with others and with God, like many other journeys, is travelled more surely with the help of a guide.

Imagine you are about to set out on a hiking holiday

over some Yorkshire moorland. You know there are tracks of marshy ground to cover, almost hidden potholes and large areas of isolated, arid territory at the centre. However, you're determined to get there. The lure of the beauty of the place makes you willing to forfeit a lot of comfort to glimpse it. You've heard about gaunt crags and the wide spaces which seem at once to shelter and to give a sense of togetherness. People have spoken of the high skies with banking clouds and the haunting cries of the birds which call you to enjoy a freedom like theirs. You want all that. But, whatever the strength of your determination, you'd be a little shortsighted if you passed up the offer of a chat with someone who knows the area and can give you some guidance; what pitfalls to look out for, spots where the lethal marsh is almost hidden. You might also be persuaded to take note of the Ordnance Survey map of the area, or even to pack it with your things for the journey.

A spiritual guide is not an expert, merely a fellow traveller who has perhaps been along a bit of the track before or has become more familiar with some of the terrain than you have yet. He or she can be of invaluable help if you ask for advice. Often the most useful thing a spiritual guide can do is to restore a sense of proportion when it looks as if you might be near to getting lost. It's a case of, "Oh those hiking boots aren't sensible at all – much too heavy" or a gentle, "There's a little further to go" in response to your jubilant cry of, "I'm there, I'm there!" uttered two or three steps onto the moor. Another wonderful gift of a guide is to make us laugh at ourselves when we're in danger of getting a bit pompous about it all. It's a great relief to be able to admit, "Ah yes, I was going round in circles there," or, "Thank-you for the tin opener. I always thought you had to open cans with your nails up to now." Laughter is one of the best indicators of humility. If we can laugh at ourselves then we don't have to defend our dignity. This in turn means we no longer regard ourselves as the all-important centre of the universe.

How to choose a guide

Sometimes contact with a contemplative community can be helpful for a while to give bearings. But some people wouldn't find that attractive or, if attractive, not possible because of circumstances. If this is the case then you could ask the Holy Spirit to help you look out for a person to guide you. Such a person should show discernment and the wisdom that comes from this. He or she should be able to listen and to sift what they hear and what is unspoken. The best guides display a naturalness; there's nothing forced about their spirituality. This naturalness is the humility which results from closeness to God. A truly humble guide will prefer your progress to his popularity and may, from time to time, teach you or tell you things which are not instantly attractive. For this reason, it's better not to choose a close friend as a guide for both the friend and you may find some of the honesty required in spiritual direction rather straining of the other aspects of your friendship.

Salt is essential to life and as Jesus said, it's the salt that gives savour. But too much salt becomes unhealthy, and in certain circumstances can kill. Spiritual guidance is like salt. Little and well savoured, thoroughly worked through, flavouring all of your life, is the right amount. Too much can lead to a reliance on the guide rather than on God (lethal) or can encourage a false intensity, when you find yourself dredging up something to say which is interesting. Too much can also encourage an inflation of the self-importance – self-revelation is a heady wine. It's easy to fall into the trap of living in order to talk about it rather than talking to clarify the living.

Despite the note of caution, the advantages of spiritual guidance far outweigh the possible pitfalls. Sometimes the guide moves what to him is a little finger, hardly raised, but the movement points the traveller to an entirely new signpost and pathway. This happened for me several years ago. During a time of wordless intercession I suddenly felt threatened by a powerful, unfixed presence of evil. I tried to stick with the silence but my being before God was blotted out by the sense of unsafety and fear. The following day I rang my spiritual director. "Just go back to some form of set prayer said slowly and with attention," she counselled. "It's a good way to steady you and it provides a pathway for the Holy Spirit to enter the situation with more power. Your attention can't be focused on your feelings if you're slowly repeating strong, God-filled words." She was right. The sense of evil had pulled me away from being silent before God. A prayer loved by Christians down the centuries provided a wall of protection once more. I used the "Our Father".

Another time a friend greatly abused her friendship with me. My guide said two things. Firstly, "Lots of praise." Then she added, "Lots of compassion." Again this was exactly what I needed to hear. The lots of praise provided a life jacket which I put on to save me from drowning in my own hurt and preoccupation with the situation. As I praised, the Holy Spirit was able to tug me into some sense of proportion again. The lots of compassion opened up the hitherto ignored sense of my friend's humanity and weakness which is the same as my humanity and weakness. It created bonds once more. I understood that she and I were much the same. Our ability to forgive is rooted in an experience of our shared condition which comes when we get a glimpse of God's mercy which folds over all of us.

Confessing your sins

The area of spiritual guidance is linked with what some churches have, until recently, called "confession". This is now renamed "reconciliation" which is a much more accurate description of what it is about. So powerful is the relief and the help from God's Spirit that we receive when we admit our need that even a request for a blessing can change a life.

Caterina Fiesca Adorna, a young, unhappily married and lonely woman, lived in Genoa in the fifteenth century.

Her husband lurched from affair to affair and left her mainly to her own devices. For months she tried to dream up ways of escaping from the monotony and isolation of her life. In desperation, she even prayed that she'd become ill and be confined to bed for three months, anything to drum up a little support and sympathy. Her sister grew increasingly worried about her state of mind and suggested the only spiritual therapy that she knew was available. "Why don't you go to confession?" she urged.

As much for want of something to do as anything else, Catherine agreed. But she wouldn't go to confession, she was too shy and her emotions too raw for that. All the bravery she could muster was to say she'd go to a priest for a blessing.

A few days later, she sidled into one of the town's churches, searched for a priest and, mechanically, knelt down in front of him. In apathy and loneliness, she crouched there. As the priest pronounced the blessing of God over her, his words formed a beam down which streamed the light and life of God. Willingness of even so reluctant a kind had opened the doors of her inner life, and now God's love poured in.

Hardly able to take in what was happening, and weak with the eruption of life at the centre of her being, she knelt there and muttered, "No more world; no more sin." Then, in amazement and gratitude, "Oh, Love, can it be that thou hast called me with so much love and revealed to me at one view what no tongue can describe?"

A few minutes later, she stumbled home. From then on, like Jesus, she returned again and again to the source of the abundant love. She became known throughout Genoa for her prayerful wisdom and as the love of God is always extending its compassion, she responded to the appalling conditions of her city at that time by building and running a hospital for victims of the plague.

You may have no experience of the form of reconciliation practised in some churches or you may not feel comfortable taking part in it. Nevertheless, confession to a friend (again, perhaps, not too intimate a friend and one who can be trusted to be beyond both shock and gossip) can be of enormous help in opening us up to the love of God at levels we've not been aware of before. It is important to know that you are forgiven and even to find a gesture that makes this plain to the less accessible levels of your personality. One way might be to write down what you want to talk about, or at least some indication of it. The friend can affirm God's love and forgiveness and, as a symbol of this, tear up the paper or burn it. We need to accept that our sin is consumed in the flames of God's love. Like all knowledge that changes us, this is not an intellectual experience but a response of heart and spirit. Another way to assure yourself of forgiveness is to imagine Jesus standing in front of you looking at you with love and enjoyment. Feel him breathe his forgiveness over you and into the depths of your life. Breathe in that forgiveness and breathe out your thanks.

Experiencing forgiveness urges me on to freedom. I'm encouraged to be what I am; the image of God. It also gives me strength against temptation because it reminds me not to take lightly the astonishing mercy of God.

Retreats

In many parts of Christ's Church, there has long been a tradition of travelling the journey of prayer together. Some choose to spend their lives doing this and enter one of the special communities devoted to such an activity. Most monasteries provide facilities for guests and from time to time it can be a very helpful experience to spend a day or two in such an atmosphere. Like the smile that ripples through an audience when they catch on to a witticism, something of the stillness and offering of love ripples out to the visitor. Just as one has smiled, so one is stilled and helped to offer worship by the company of such people and by the atmosphere which has developed through continued prayer.

A few weeks back, I was chatting with another parent at the school gates while we waited for our children to trickle

out. He started to tell me something of his experience of a
retreat he'd been on recently. He is a member of the
Pentecostal fellowship in town and said that he hadn't
been sure what a retreat was. However, he felt like a break
and liked the sound of the place, so he booked in for the
weekend. What he hadn't realised was that the entire two
days would be silent. He said the silence was horrible at
first – it made him self-aware and clumsy. At supper on the
Friday evening, the sound of his cup when he replaced it
on the saucer was like the roar of a cannon. In the end, he
left half the drink.

The first meditation relaxed him a little and in his room
later he picked up his Bible for his usual evening reading.
The reading went much the same as ever but, when he
started to pray, he was surprised to find he wanted to
spend much more time than he was used to in worship. The
next morning he woke up to a stronger pull to praise than
he'd ever experienced. He knelt in silence until breakfast.
As the weekend continued he found that the silence which
had at first felt like a strait-jacket was now beginning to fit
him comfortably like something tailor made. "Been home
a week now," he said. "Funny thing, I always used to have
the radio on as background. Now I find it irritating. I want
the silence. Things seem to be growing from it."

We couldn't speak further because class five tumbled
into the playground and his son ran up to him full of news
of the football last lesson.

Places for prayer

Jesus seems to have felt that choice of place was important
in prayer. When he wanted to be alone with his Father,
resting in his love, we read again and again, "He went up
to the hills to pray." Some people aren't finely tuned to
place but others are. If you respond to atmosphere or to
architecture and tradition, then going to pray in a place
where prayer has been offered down the generations will
help. The residue of offered prayer will itself still thought
and be an invitation to enter into worship.

Some of the Christians in Canterbury meet together every couple of months for a "Celebration". This is a service of worship and teaching where the gifts of the Spirit are often in evidence. On one occasion last year the Dean and Chapter kindly lent the Cathedral for the service. In May David Pytches came to speak to a packed nave. I arrived a little early and sat by a gentleman and his wife I hadn't seen before. We struck up a conversation. "We've come in from Herne Bay," the man said and then added, "We're Baptists." Later he confided, "I always love it here. You can sort of feel the prayer of all those past Christians, can't you?"

When you pray at home you may find it helpful to build up your own residue of prayer by trying, as much as possible, to use the same place for reading the Bible and praying. Then, when you come to pray, your spirit will spring to the habit of attention and worship which it associates with that part of the house or room. We are not disembodied spirits; we are people and we need to use our physicality, its senses and habits, as means to respond to God. We come to God through our bodies and his created universe, not by passing them. The more we are at home as people, the more we can appreciate other forms of creation and other worlds.

Thank you for life in the world
Thank you for your Word in the world
Thank you for worlds beyond words
Help us to enter your stillness.

5

TRAVELLING LIGHT

One of our daughters has just become a teenager. If I ask her why she's wearing blue eyeshadow, I get a reply along the lines of, "Oh, Everyone does."

"And why do you like . . . whoever the pop idol is?"

"He's the greatest!"

"Who says so?"

"Oh, Everyone."

Everyone seems suddenly to have loomed very large in her life. I only have to look at her to know that Everyone's wearing shorter skirts now and that Everyone's into pink. Everyone's got a Walkman and Everyone stays up until all hours.

We only grow through relationship. I am only I when I am conscious there's a you. In a rudimentary but important way, that's what all Catherine's references to "Everyone" are saying. Our daughter feels she is only alive in so far as she is approved of by other teenagers.

Being who you are

In the spiritual journey, relating is just as important but that importance takes rather a different form. Its form is several stages on from the importance of "Everyone". Having lived through our "Everyone" phase and then having experienced something of the love of God for me specially, I've gained enough security to ask, not, "What does everyone think of me?" but, rather, "What do I want?" In the journey towards God I can also ask, "Which routes?" and "What speed?"

It's very important that we listen to the Holy Spirit about these questions. We all love to codify, simplify and make rules. It allays anxiety – the old "I know where I am" type of security again. It also helps us to define ourselves by excluding others. Other people also like to impose rules on us and we can find that a pressure hard to resist. But all this carefulness and neatness melts in the fire of the love of God. The Lord calls us to rejoice in our uniqueness. If we are afraid to explore our uniqueness then we don't understand the creativity of love, nor have we yet appreciated how much God rejoices in each one of us. The beauty of a garden consists of a harmony achieved through the diversity of its plants. It does not consist in a boring, clone similarity. If we were all roses, sooner or later, we'd give our eye teeth for a sight or smell of a honeysuckle.

If five minutes a day of coming to the Lord in love is all you can manage, then that's fine. Equally, there's nothing wrong, and you're not mad, if you have three hours a day and you can spend it in such prayer. For some people, a longer stretch on alternate days might be a comfortable rhythm. Others find that the cycles of their activity and reflection move more slowly. Several months of activity may arise from previous weeks or months of relative inactivity. Your daily body clock is important too. You're not helping the Holy Spirit if you choose the frayed ends of the day in which to go into silence. Spiritual abilities are probably tattered then too and silence ushers in either a hundred and one clamouring thoughts or the heaviness of a weary spirit which is far from a worshipful alertness of quiet love.

We all have different characteristics, and whereas reading may be a favoured preparation for prayer for one person, you are under no obligation to conform to the favoured methods of your friends or church leaders. In prayer as in many things, "One man's meat is another man's poison."

Patience

Although you may not want to express your love and worship with too much physicality, all of us are physical expressions of personality in a physical universe, and we can't leave ourselves as bodies out of worship altogether. Perhaps we find an upturned face eager for the grace of the Lord, an outstretched arm portraying our longing and emptiness or a deep bow of wonder before the awful wholeness of God a fitting start to our time of silence.

We need something of the infinite patience of God with ourselves during our time of prayer. The reason I mention this directly after a brief word about the body at prayer is because any self-consciousness is a falling short of love. Love is always going out from itself in compassion and celebration and is far too concerned with another to be conscious of self. Our most obvious expression of self-consciousness is our embarrassment with ourselves as bodies. This blocks our patience with and delight in ourselves which is the Holy Spirit's invitation to us. After all, it would be churlish of a work of art to despise itself when it came before the artist. He'd hardly feel complimented on his efforts by such a meanness of spirit. Just a little easing of our crippling bodily self-consciousness helps us to be patient with ourselves when we pray.

Relaxing in prayer

Very often we need such patience. If we've put a certain time aside for prayer then we should stick at it for that time. We are there to love God and to be open to him, not to please ourselves and to monitor or indulge our own emotions. Sometimes prayer has been little more than a holding together of my worries or preoccupations and the love of God. Nothing seems to be happening. But patience with the nothingness does its own work in carving deep inside us, chip by chip, the capacity for God which we long for. Sometimes, quite unexpectedly and suddenly, I have been surprised by peace or joy or a resting in God's love. Just as I've resigned myself to a half hour's struggle, the Lord offers me his lap as a head rest. But back to those arid half hours . . .

Staying put is not the same as forcing ourselves before

God or trying to force God. All we're doing is guarding our receptivity and our availability. We are not trying to "make things happen", or work ourselves up into a state where "things can happen". The pressure to feel that "things should happen" is great when we meet people who readily share their visions or their words with us when we've had no visions or words or when, recently, God has not communicated in such ways with us. But St. Paul told us our job is "to rejoice with those who rejoice". Doing this does not mean that we should be having the same experiences, any more than it means we should cut ourselves off from others who seem to be rich, when we are feeling spiritually poverty stricken. The old spiritual laws come into play again:

1) Our uniqueness is both our and God's glory.

2) We do not possess any spiritual experiences. Growth into God is growth away from possession. What we are after is the freedom which allows things to happen. We want to notice what God wants of us or others, or what God offers us or others. We then want to continue to seek the presence of the God who will be, not the static God of "I am" who might be held and then caged by us.

3) Everything that we can put into words about the prayer of being there for God is only the tip of the flame. The burning fire lies deep within. It is this fire, which we cannot communicate through words or pictures, which transforms us into itself.

Balance

Tied up with all this is St. Paul's rather stern reminder that, "It is for prophets to control prophetic inspiration, for the God who inspires them is not a God of disorder but of peace." (1 Corinthians 14:32) St. Paul reminds us that the touchstone of our life of prayer lies not in sensations but in relations. Some people who are finely tuned psychologically can easily get swamped by spiritual experiences and become unable to "switch off". Although at times this may occur quite legitimately as a side effect of a special work of God in us, it shouldn't be the norm. The Lord desires us to have his integration, which means a balance between psychological and spiritual responses should be kept. It's a danger signal if we find ourselves see-sawing round in all sorts of experiences which we say we can't control.

God's love does not force us. When we're babies we may experience the fits and starts, wails, giggles and un-directed energies of babies. But, as we grow a little, then the various aspects of our personality should start to knit together into a greater, not a lesser, harmony. The Lord our God is one, and we are made in his image of dynamic wholeness. Little by little, at increasing depths, the Holy Spirit is wooing us into his harmony. So, romping among our spiritual sensations and letting them romp all over us is the hallmark of spiritual toddlerdom. It's a little like the two year old, who, having recently discovered his navel, is fascinated with it and insists on showing it to friend and stranger alike.

Letting go

Another sign of strain is the sort of super-spirituality which can become a burden to us and to everyone else. It's a wearing thing to create an image and then try to live up to it. It is God who invents us, not we ourselves. If we insist on inventing and then guarding our own image, then we lose our enjoyment of other people. We use them to bolster up our idea of ourselves. With the name of the Lord frequently on our lips we re-enact the dramas of Lucifer and Adam. This is all that sin is – it's not allowing things or people their own lives but making them an object in MY universe. How often do I ring people up and enquire, "How are you?" not because I care and want to know but because that's a polite manipulation? I want them to think I care so that they'll feel warm towards me and be receptive to the request which is the real reason for my phone call. We have a host of ways tucked up our sleeves to hook people into the net of our self-comfort. It's quite difficult to become aware of them, lay them down and remain forgiving of those who continue to manipulate us.

God the Father, Son and Spirit live in an equal relationship. No one loves more than the other, no one offers more and no one receives more. Yet all are indispensable in the One. All are the One.

In Heaven, each of the saints glories in the achievements and gifts of the others. Each feels enriched by the others, each contributes to the others. Each is indispensable. Heaven is the fullness of the picture of God.

The trouble with being super-spiritual is that we cut ourselves off from all that joy. We can only appreciate people if they "need" us or if we can clock them into our scheme as being at least one rung, and preferably two, lower than us on the spiritual ladder. When we experience people as rivals it is because we are defending some aspect of our lives or of our image of ourselves which we have carefully constructed.

Often those with the most fruitful ministries are those to whom any such ministry is incidental. They are so absorbed by God and by God in others that they haven't the self-consciousness to describe themselves in terms of role or work or influence. They are too busy enjoying others to think in terms of influencing them.

I always know if I am spiritually sick. The sure indication is when I start to tot up who I am, what I've achieved, what I've got and what I plan. I take my eyes from celebrating the Lord and swivel them round to me and a world with me at its centre. Such thinking of course, opens the flood gates to anxiety. For, if I've "got" all this, then I can lose it too, can't I? Or others may be out to rob me of it. Mary, the mother of Jesus, described this state of mind most accurately in her song of thanksgiving to God when she declared, "The arrogant of heart and mind he has put to rout". (Luke 1:51) It reads even more graphically in the King James' Version of the Bible, "He has scattered the proud in the imagination of their hearts." Any wresting after super-spirituality is a failure to travel light. We've

picked up the oppressive burden of our own self-esteem
again.

> Lord of lightness, you dance through the universe in
>   laughter and rejoicing
> And I glimpse the heels of your dancing.
> Help me to come to you in lightness of heart and life.

PART TWO

FURTHER IN

6

THE FOOD OF LOVE

"The Sound of Music is on," the girls told David when he walked into the sitting room just before Christmas.

"Not again!" he exclaimed and strode out as quickly as possible.

They remained glued to the set for the entire film. I was busy making mince pies and then sorting out the wrapping paper for the last of the presents. I had to go through the sitting room to the study to get some Sellotape. Just at that moment Catherine's "Ah" of satisfaction attracted my attention. I stopped to watch for a moment or two.

The scene was the great ball called by the Baron Von Trapp to impress his house guests. Women in long, gracious dresses danced with men in tails in an Austrian grand house of unstinted pre-War elegance. Maria, the children's much loved governess, watched the dancing with the seven children from outside. It was a balmy summer's evening and they gathered on the terrace to press noses against the glass of the great french windows. Inside, the men and women whirled and waltzed and drank champagne. Then the small orchestra struck up another tune. "It's an old Austrian folk dance," Maria told the children.

"D'you know how to do it?" the eldest boy asked her.

"Yes."

"Show me."

"All right."

So Maria took the boy for her partner and started to count out, "One, two, three – this way."

The teenager tried to follow but made rather an awkward turn.

Unnoticed by them, the Baron has left the dancing inside and is watching this from a position just behind the children. Now he steps forward, taps his son on the shoulder with one immaculately gloved hand and, while Maria is still not sure what is happening, partners her for the dance.

The first swift movements flow past and then the couple come to the slower mid section of the dance. They move hand in hand, closer now, face to face. Eye catches eye. Diffidently, he smiles. She blushes. Feet slow. Time slows, draws itself out, halts. They gaze at each other, unaware of the children. It is the recognition of love. The sparks of connection which for weeks have darted and retreated, or have jigged at the edges of their lives, flow together and electrify. The man and the woman will not again be the same. Nothing will again be the same . . .

I once heard an interview on the radio between a sports commentator and an athlete. They talked about training, the hard work and the dedication.

"And what makes it all worthwhile?" the interviewer asked.

"It's not so much the winning."

"Oh!" the interviewer couldn't stifle his surprise.

"It's something which happens when you've been running a certain time," the athlete started to explain. "You've got your training right and you know you're on form. Then at the beginning of the race you get into the position you've worked out beforehand, if you can. You pace yourself and make sure you're tactically on schedule. Sometimes after a bit the pain starts, muscles aching and your legs heavy. That's especially bad if you haven't got the breathing right. But then, without warning, you crash through the pain barrier, or rather, what seemed a barrier just melts away, and the whole thing becomes so effortless. That's great. You have the sense you could run and run and never grow tired. Your body does exactly what you want it to. Everything about the running is you, and you are the running. It's not always like that, of course, and you never know when it's going to happen. But it's the best feeling in the world when it does."

Are there any similarities between these two experiences?

At first they may seem worlds apart. One is to do with the age-old event of boy meets girl, and the other is a solo athletic performance. The situations could hardly be more different. But let's look a little more closely at them separately.

The moment of falling in love for Maria and the Baron isn't isolated – in fact it's the pinnacle of a lot of hard work:

They have observed each other for several weeks.

They share common concerns – the children's happiness and education.

They speak the same language and have similar interests.

They've already learned to respect and appreciate each other as people.

They've glimpsed into each other's strengths and weaknesses.

They've both practised offering love for quite some time – the Baron in his first marriage and Maria in the early stages of the life of a convent and, more recently, in her imaginative care of the children.

Finally, neither of them has planned this moment. The inpouring of love is itself pure gift.

From what the athlete says, we can understand that he, too, has gone in for a lot of preparation. He's paced himself for weeks; seen exactly when to make his moves in any race; watched the competition (nowadays that probably means intensive scrutiny of reel after reel of film or video). He knows the language of his love and calls it tactics. By training he's prepared himself thoroughly for the sport, and he's developed a great deal of self-respect by doing so. He's also learned, and often the hard way, to respect other athletes. Never underestimate! He's eradicated from his life whatever doesn't fit in with his training and he's come

to terms with some of his weaknesses, so much so that he's
prepared to endure the pain barrier. He's cashed in on his
strengths – he'd be a fool not to – and for many years, he's
made all this effort as an offering of himself to what he
loves. Like Maria and the Baron he cannot plan the
moment when effort falls away and he eases into an
effortless coming together of everything about himself, so
that he and the running are the same thing. The moment
of unity in his experience is pure gift.

So, at a closer look, the two experiences have a lot in
common.

Now, let's have a quick recap of what's gone into your
response to God's invitation to "Come" so far.

You've evaluated your strengths and weaknesses with
regard to preparation for prayer.

You've put in quite a lot of training, keeping to a
discipline and, the hardest training of all, learning to obey
God's prompts towards deeper relationships with other
people.

You've started to evaluate the opposition, sifting intuitive experiences to see that they are in line with the love
of God rather than individual, sometimes unhealthy,
inner voices.

You've started to look at the Lord. There can be no love
without looking. And you've started to look at others who
are alive in him; those in the completion of Heaven and
those on earth.

You've started to learn the language of God; the
language of a knowing beyond understanding; the
language of receptive, imaginative love.

You've learned something of your weakness.

You've begun to offer in those times when staying in
stillness before the Lord is difficult and you're plagued by
distraction. Then, your obstinate being there for God,
whatever else is battering at the doors of heart and spirit,
or when prayer is stringing you out with boredom or
anxiety, is a real sacrifice of offering, love and praise.

But, at the end of all these things for Maria and the

Baron and the athlete came an unasked-for experience, richer than anything they'd prepared for. What came to them was love bringing joy and unity. And love's coming was pure gift.

Perhaps, although we're seeking God himself rather than any gift, we are now able to receive gifts. And the Lord, the Great Lover, gives in cupfuls, crushed down and flowing over and in a fullness that leaves us breathless with wonder.

What can we say about this giving? Not only are many of the best things in life free, but they also can't be talked about. By that I mean that describing them doesn't much help another person to experience the same thing. I may talk to you about the sunset I've enjoyed, describe its range of colours, the changing forms and streaking of the clouds, the flushes and glows and then gentle fadings from the sky; but how much better to say, "Come quickly and see for yourself." I hope that so far, what I've been writing has been a "Come quickly and see for yourself" book. Now I'm at the point where I might try to describe something of the experience. But I can't. So, let me do what a jeweller did once when I asked him to show me a diamond. He held it to the light and turned it slowly this way and that. Facet after facet appeared, flickered, caught life and blazed. I couldn't see the whole stone at any one time but, at the end of a few minutes' turning, I'd gained some sort of impression of the immense light, variety and depth within that single jewel.

So, without trying to show a complete experience (and no one can; we only ever start to explore God) perhaps I can share some of the facets and pray the Holy Spirit catches them into his light. I speak of "I" throughout but the "I"s are many people and the experiences are the experiences of many. The diamond of the love of God is a stone which people have sought after, dropped everything to gain, gazed at and been transformed by through the centuries. Because such experience can't really be talked about, you may find my attempt to communicate it strange and difficult reading. Like all love language it can sound

extravagant or exaggerated at times, and rather odd if
read out of context.

Facet 1

Effort drops away. I used to seek you, Lord. Now I am
sought by you. Each morning I wake to your presence
surrounding me and beckoning to me. Whether I'm baking
or studying or pushing the pram, suddenly there you are
saying again, "Come". And my spirit looks up, and runs
into your arms. Your love wakes me in the night. In the
day, it leaps through speech and writing and housework.
I am held in you, God. Your peace stretches through
me and leads me to a stillness which fills and completes
me.

Facet 2

What's happening to me physically? Quite often now I'm
incapable of standing or sitting or even kneeling to pray.
Your holiness makes me fall down before you. Increasingly, prayer is flat on my face. Sometimes I tremble and
I don't know why. My breathing automatically slows as
soon as I surrender to you. Tears fall: scalding in regret,
cooler streams of longing.

Facet 3

Once I could hardly stop thinking or feeling. Prayer was
plagued by distractions. Now there is only silence. But the
silence is filled with you, like a glass is filled with strong
wine. To think or feel is to jolt some of the dark liquid.

Facet 4

Often I glimpse a need before a person speaks. The eyes of
the spirit have developed their own sight. Like X-rays,
they penetrate the surface, the chat and small talk, and
look through to something of the centre of a person. This is

not comfortable and I am pleased when my eye winks or closes.

Facet 5

It is in silence and in stillness that deep calls to deep. I want the company of very few people now. Lord, when people come they drop into the pool of your love, and when they go the waters of the pool close over the memory. People are neither a necessity nor an intrusion. But, below the comings and goings, the desire to be alone with you throbs and aches in me like a wound.

Facet 6

The joy is uncontainable. If someone speaks your name, Lord, the name Jesus, then I look down for fear I'll laugh with delight or hug them.

Facet 7

What has happened to time, Lord? Where does it go? There is never enough. Being loved by you and loving you stretches through the hours, and then contracts them to a single point of no time. Where there is love, time falls away which is why you, Lord, are eternal. For you are love. If love fails, there will only be the filling up of days.

Facet 8

There are no longer two worlds. The earthly and the heavenly are intermingled. I walk into the street and see cars parked on either side of the road. I also see Heaven and Hell, and the spiritual battles in high places.

Facet 9

When I walk in the street I look into the faces of people. And the people are different. You are in all of them, God.

They are alive only in you. They are your image. Everyone
is himself and everyone is part of you.

Facet 10

Now I understand why theology is not worked out just by
thinking. Theology is reflection on the experience of you
forged through prayer. Language is the only means we
have of trying to make sense of our experience for others.
But it's a poor tool. I can't think my way to understand
you. You, of your mercy, give me understanding.

Facet 11

I try to think about you, Lord. I try to use symbols as I used
to. I try to see you in streams and hills and the rest of your
creation and in what I read. But it's difficult. There's a pull
beyond all this. It's as if the sun's come out and is blazing
through the sky. It eats up all the lesser lights in its
shining.

Facet 12

How much of this can I take? I am not worthy. Oh God, you
are too good. This is too rich.

Facet 13

I desire more. I hardly know you. You are all that matters.
Nothing else is of importance. I have everything in
you, and yet the desire for more of you aches through
me. I'm complete and I'm hungry. I see and I'm happily
blinded.

Facet 14

Doesn't love like this kill you in the end?

Facet 15

I have not enough to give. I have nothing to give. My God, when will I cease and your life only leap in the world?

Facet 16

Now I understand why scripture is written in the way it is. Jesus told stories; Jesus spoke in paradox; Jesus questioned. And Jesus was silent. All these forms of communication reflect you. Thinking about you apart from experiencing you is like trying to coat a diamond with dust, and then saying, "Look. See. There it is. There's the shine!" The diamond shakes itself and the dust of concepts falls from it.

Facet 17

Yours is the power, Lord. Your glory fills me with dread. You hold everything that is and was and is to come in the palm of your hand. You search me and I am nothing. Why does your presence not burn me up?

Facet 18

I choose to be nothing. My nothingness is swallowed up in the immensity of your love. The greatest terror left is the fear of losing you.

Facet 19

The silence is full of you. The silence rejoices; it whispers; it encourages and it holds. It is everything. Words are only words: dead flat things, cold fish, beside such a leaping flame of silence.

Facet 20

Questions drop away. I've always loved questions. I'm plagued by the desire for meaning and scourged by the

lack of it. Now I know love is its own meaning. Where
there is love there are no more reasons.

Facet 21

All suffering – all my suffering (but dare I speak for
others?) is part of a wholeness. In a way I can't understand
but experience, all is well. Your peace unfurls in me.
Everything is connected: everything is mine. As St. Paul
said, ". . . the world, life, and death, the present and the
future, all of them belong to you – yet you belong to Christ,
and Christ to God." (1 Corinthians 3:23)

Facet 22

Now I know why the epistles say we were chosen before
the world began. The created is formed in the uncreated.
Time is swallowed by the eternal moment. How can all
not have been chosen? How can all not be brought to
completion?

Facet 23

Come, Lord, come. When will I see your face? When will I
wake up and be like you?

. . . .

Now, what can we draw from that about the work of God in
such prayer?
    Firstly, the utterances are the words of a love song.
Perhaps it's a little, feeble echo of the eternal love song
within the Trinity. Our response to immense love is to
offer ourselves. That is part of what we mean by saying
we're made in the image of God. As the Son is always
offering and receiving, so the more we offer, the more we
contact joy. This is why Jesus told us that if we want to
save our lives, we should first lose them. Joy is what we are
created for. As we travel further out from ourself towards
being truly a person, so we experience more joy. God is

eternally generous and any generosity on our part is
rewarded with an outpouring of his love. Generosity can
take small, hidden forms. A friend told me of one morning
when her husband said he'd ring a distant member of the
family to wish him "Happy Birthday", a meanness in her
remembered, "You did that last year and he didn't ring you
on your birthday. He won't remember this year, either."
She didn't speak the thought out loud but almost burnt the
toast whilst battling against the meanness. As soon as she
decided to keep quiet, not only did the peace of God return
but she said she felt affection, for the first time in many
months, for that cousin. All we have to do is to move out of
the way to let God's generosity through. The first person to
benefit is nearly always ourselves.

How does the silence relate to other forms of praise, such
as speaking or singing in tongues?

For many years I had no one to compare experiences
with. I only knew that to be held by God in a wordless love
was, for me, far greater than to speak, even with the praise
of tongues (although I sometimes used tongues in intercession). In fact, any sort of speech in prayer became an
interference. Better than this, the experience of God in
silence persisted whatever else I was doing, whereas
specifically spoken or sung praise faded when the speaking or singing stopped.

Then, when we were living in Maidstone, a speaker
came to the annual week of Bible teaching held in town.
He was from Birmingham and spent some time in one of
his talks describing the experience of worship in his
church. He said that during one evening service the entire
congregation praised God in singing and then in the
singing of tongues. Gradually a silence fell and, in that
silence, the worship deepened to a far greater degree than
during the singing. So I realised that many of us experienced the relative depths of spoken and sung praise and
the adoration of the Lord that goes beyond words.

Once the spirit starts to leap in love towards its source
then it's sensitive to any stimulus from that love, just as
when we love a person we're sensitive to any mention of

the name. Also, when we love a person, our life takes on a richness in his or her presence. In fact lovers are notorious not only for pondering the name of the beloved but also for trying to imprint that name wherever they can. Hence the "Juliet" in a heart on the park bench, and the fading, but still discernible "Mary" scratched into a tree trunk. Some people find that once they become sensitive to the love of God, then the mention of his name evokes a response from them. St. Catherine of Genoa was like this. When she was looking after the sick in her hospital, she came across a woman dying of the plague. Through swollen, cracked lips, the dying woman uttered the name "Jesus". Knowing that the disease was fearfully catching, but unable to stop herself when she heard the name, Catherine stooped down and kissed the woman on the lips. Sure enough, she caught the plague. She didn't die, however. When love is evoked like this, the systematic reading of scripture can be quite difficult. We read something like "The Word became flesh" and can go no further. We are swept up into the wonder of that statement. Our hearts are flamed to worship and we find it difficult not to stop for silent love.

Reading the Bible

But the continued reading of the Bible and, if possible, the feeding of our minds and hearts through meditation and imaginative response to the word of God is essential. Such continued reading achieves several things, among them:

1) It helps to stop us becoming individualistic in our faith. The history of the Church is scattered with the cul de sac teachings of those whose often profound experience of God has been wrenched away from the anchor of community and scripture into their own new doctrines. This can sometimes happen when the gift of prophecy is used without understanding. Then people drift away through pride or ignorance into yet another branch of the Church, or sect.

2) It helps to keep or, if necessary, restore the balance

between the intellectual, imaginative and emotional response to God. At some time in our development we may experience the predominance of some aspects of our personality in our love of God but the Holy Spirit, whilst using these as springboards, is gently leading us towards a more integrated offering of ourselves. All lovers are "off balance" from time to time. Experiences can be heady but growth depends on integrating such experiences into the whole of our lives, not in losing them or being flooded by them. If we lose our love, divorce takes place or, in the Christian life, indifference. If we are flooded by our experience for any length of time then self-indulgence may become the norm. Then we fall in love with love and, in the spiritual life, we seek our own feelings rather than the will of God.

3) Continued study of scripture and meeting with other Christians reminds us that the touchstone of all our journeying is the quality of our relationships and not of our sensations. As St. Teresa of Avila, a great woman of prayer and a very down-to-earth lady, said tartly, "I cannot know if I love God but I can know if I love my fellow men."

4) Experiences ebb and flow and God is speaking to us in the ebbs and the flows. If, when we feel rich in the Lord, we abandon our usual disciplines of reading or study and praying with others, what will be left for the times when we don't sense his presence? Very soon, only our own feelings. Then, when he's "not there", we just give up.

I wasn't surprised to learn that in those churches where God is performing physical healing, the leadership is increasingly concerned that the Church should learn to worship. The gifts of the Holy Spirit flow from a depth of worship of the Giver. That is why we must not become over-curious or over-excited about the gifts in themselves. What they are is a visible sign or outworking of a new quality of life. The quality of life is the life of God which is always seeking to bring wholeness in all its forms. The life of God is unstoppable, and it is by worship that we put ourselves in the flow of the stream of that life.

So, in our own lives, once we really respond to the love of
God, his gifts become a kind of cherished incidental to our
worship. God gives them so that we may be useful to other
people. We don't need them for our own satisfaction. That
is why St. Paul says that the gift of tongues is the lowest of
the gifts. It's the one which is least useful to anyone else. It
is not surprising that depth of worship is the soil in which
the fruit of the higher gifts flourishes. It is these gifts
which are of most use to others.

Life and death

Shining from the facets was a longing to be taken up into
God – to see him face to face; to wake up like him. All this
echoes the longings in scripture, "I shall see thy face, and
be blessed with a vision of thee when I awake." (Psalm
17:15) and, "Now we see only puzzling reflections in a
mirror, but then we shall see face to face." (1 Corinthians
13:12) A strong experience of the presence of God often
ushers in a great deal of thought about death. This is not
morbid. It is in tune with the facts of our lives as they are.
"All mortals are like grass; all their splendour like the
flower of the field; the grass withers, the flower falls." (1
Peter 1:24) Also, as part of our growing response to God,
we've become aware of those who have died in faith. The
letter to the Hebrews calls them witnesses to faith, around
us like a cloud. They live in the continual presence of God,
and so they are much more alive than we are. They love
and worship their Lord, and they love and care about us.
So death, which might have seemed like a great divide,
has already diminished to the proportions of a screen
temporarily cutting off one section of the room from
another. Besides which, when we love God, the real divide
is not so much that between life and death but more that
between moving closer or ignoring him. It is this which
starts to haunt and direct our lives.

You are alive, and one day you will be dead. Imagine
yourself given the opportunity to look back at your life just
moments before you die. What has been most important to

you? What would you want to be remembered for? Who would you want to remember you? What have you done? What do you wish you had done?

Now return to the present and, in the light of your response to the questions, jot down some guidelines to future priorities.

What does the fact that you will die say to you about how to live your life? To me it says, "Never mind the width, feel the quality." Quite often when my life is most busy or, from the outside, looks most fulfilled or interesting, I am aware of a disconnection between the various activities themselves and, more importantly, between the volume of activity and the life of God in me. Loving God may mean cutting down. When I no longer have time for God, then I am no longer alive: I am only existing. I would like to learn increasingly about how to live through time with the values of eternity. In the end, all that will remain of me is love. In the end, the only question about the activity of my life is the question, "How much did you love?"

Knowing that I will die makes me want to live each moment to the full; not in the sense of squeezing it dry, like an orange, but in the sense of letting each moment be of value for me. Do I ignore those I love? Do I daydream the hours away? Do I hold grudges? Life is too short. "God" is a "now" word inviting me to love more fully *now* as he is willing to fill every moment with his love.

But there's more than that, isn't there, in the longings of those who pray? Sometimes they yearn for death. This is the opposite of what most of us feel. We fear leaving everything that is familiar to us on earth or that we love on earth. But, for some, it seems death is not a separation from what they love, it is the longed-for journey bringing them closer to their Love. Death is the fullness of love.

The healing of wholeness

We cannot journey closer to God and not experience some healing. God is holy. The word "holy" comes from the same root as "whole". So, when God beckons us, he beckons us into his wholeness. His wholeness is love: it is love which heals.

It's as if you're in a hot country walking with bare feet over baked, cracked land. You are thirsty and dusty, and flies buzz round you annoyingly. You don't find walking easy at the best of times because, for years now, you've had a limp. It's a kind of stiffness in your left leg; the result of a horrible experience when you were younger. It doesn't incapacitate you completely. You can go for months without feeling too much pain but then, for no apparent reason, it plays up again and you're aware of it for perhaps a week at a time. Of course, if anyone knocks it then sharp fingers of pain jab jagged nails up and down you, all over again.

The pain's quite bad at the moment. You've been on the leg too much recently and your general weariness doesn't help.

But what's this ahead of you? There seem to be some trees, and between the trees you can glimpse water. Water; cool water, you hope. You are nearer now and can hear something. It's the splashing of water over and over, like the repeated notes of a song. Not only a pool but, behind the trees and the pool, a cascading waterfall. Individual drops glisten in the light like sequins and, when the sun catches them, it paints a dazzling rainbow through the haze.

Your feet pad more lightly now over the parched earth. You can hardly feel the pain in your leg although you're managing to work up quite a pace. Your tongue flickers over dry lips. How long before I feel the coolness? How long before I can drink?

At last, you're there. You're about to flop down by the pool when a voice calls out "Come".

Despite your thirst, you look up. The voice is so inviting.

"Come", it urges from the direction of the waterfall.

So you stagger on the last few steps. The fall is not a cascade over solid rocks but gentler than that. It rills and trips down to dance on a ledge of rock at its base. You step onto the base.

The water tumbles over you. It washes away the dirt

and the dust. First you can see rivulets of clean gleaming over your skin, then whole areas of glistening skin. Your hair swings free of clogging mud. Your limbs feel light in the water. You turn your face up to its song. The notes drop gently over your eyes and down your cheeks.

You open your mouth. The parched lips soften and ease. Your mouth is full of refreshing, bubbling water. It flows down your throat. The stream is in you and around you, flowing over you and through you. It cleans you and refreshes. You relax. You hear yourself laughing for pleasure and relief and joy. You're not quite sure why. But it's enough and you laugh again. Everything is all right.

Perhaps such a picture gives us the tiniest idea of the power, cleansing and gentleness of the healing of God. He enters and surrounds us when we come before him. His Spirit may lead some towards healing of past experiences. Then, under the cleansing waterfall, they retrace their lives to the point of suffering and re-live as much of that suffering as becomes available to them. But, this time, the power of God in Jesus stands beside them in the experience. The suffering is re-lived in the healing presence of God. For some this process isn't necessary. Just coming to the Lord in silence, and drinking in his love, is enough. Love surrounding and filling them eases away the deep pain of the years.

But what about hurts that cause a limp for life? What about incest, divorce, bereavement, infertility? And there are others. One day I was meditating on Jesus' resurrection appearances to his disciples, as preparation for prayer. Thomas had said that he wouldn't believe that God had raised Jesus from the dead unless he felt the wounds of the crucifixion with his own hands. Jesus appeared and said to them all, "Peace be with you!" and then to Thomas, "Reach your finger here; see my hands. Reach your hand here and put it into my side." (John 20:26–27)

Quite suddenly, it dawned on me that when God raised Jesus from the dead, he didn't cancel out the crucifixion. The crucifixion was completed in the resurrection, not

reversed. For all eternity the glorious body of Jesus blazes
with the scars of suffering. His suffering is not reversed by
his glory but is taken up into his glory. It is part of that
glory.

So, I realised, wounds for life can be transformed.
Perhaps they still hurt from time to time – and there's no
throb like the pulsing agony of a twenty-year-old wound –
perhaps grieving continues and there are no cancellings
out. But my hurts can shine. I may cry out because of them
but they need not cripple me. The power of God's Spirit can
glorify them.

I no longer feel guilty about certain deep hurts which
still hurt. Nor do I respond to slick promises along the
lines that everything can be made as if it hadn't been. I
note the hurts; bring them to God; don't feel I ought to get
over them and carry on. They may make me stumble
occasionally but the Lord can stop me falling completely.
And, in their own way, the deepest hurts, although never
good in themselves, can be the spur to prod me to turn
again and again to God. Increasingly, they are for me a
part of the conviction that, in God, all is well. Increasingly,
I experience connection between suffering and love.
Realising such a connection brings great freedom. Taking
account of the hurts, and taking them into his love, Jesus
says to me, "Peace be with you."

Suffering love

But there's another connection between suffering and love
and, this time, it's the love that of its own free will chooses
suffering. That is what Jesus did. The Son put aside the
glory he had shared with the Father before the world
began in order to become like those he loved. That is what
love always does. It works out ways of sharing the experience and the concern of those who are loved. The question
love always asks itself is, "I wonder what it feels like to
be . . . ?" And then, even if becoming like the beloved
means you go with your eyes open into voluntary loss,
then so be it, you go. In a way any sort of loving involves

the suffering of loss. To love is to lose your self-sufficiency. Once you love you are vulnerable to hurt.

Because love involved the loss and suffering for Jesus of the whole of his life and then of his death, sometimes those who learn to be still enough to understand something of that love, desire to suffer. Such a desire is a tying of the bonds of sympathy. More than most of us, Mary the mother of Jesus knew about that. For her, to love her son was to suffer. And she was told so when he was a baby in her arms, only a few days old. In the Temple Simeon explained to her, "This child is destined to be a sign which men reject; and you too shall be pierced to the heart." (Luke 2:34)

Suffering is not good in itself but, given the way the world is, suffering love is God's chosen means of redemption. It was as I started to explore this that I came nearer to understanding one of the sayings of St. Paul that had set me journeying in the first place. St. Paul shows the desire to experience what the Lord had experienced when he took our personhood on him. "It is now my happiness to suffer for you. This is my way of helping to complete, in my poor human flesh, the full tale of Christ's afflictions still to be endured, for the sake of his body which is the church." (Colossians 1:24) That desire is spiritual dynamite for it is the opposite of how most of us act most of the time. We run a mile from the possibility of being hurt and work out our defence mechanisms to an exact degree. If, by some chance, someone at last penetrates them we're hot foot on the trail of getting our own back or, at best, of closing in on ourselves once more. Not only does the Bible tell us to forgive those who hurt us but St. Paul, in his letter to the Colossians, seems actually to be courting suffering. Even more worrying, unnamed suffering at that.

In a daydream we might think of a fairly dramatic form of suffering we could choose. There's something fine about obvious martyrdom. After all, the blood of the martyrs has always been the seed of the Church. But what about suffering we'd never even thought about? What about un-dramatic, unknown suffering? What about this unknown

suffering going on as far as we can see, indefinitely?
That's not so much death by the sword but death by
the irritation of thousands of gnat bites and it doesn't hold
out much glamour. Am I willing to love God enough to
court the boredom of an inflexible daily routine? Do I seek
out the company of someone I know who's got a rough
tongue? Do I joyfully look for inconvenience and then offer
it to God so that, in the fullness of time, all shall be well
when the incompleteness of time is healed in the fullness
of eternity? Do I court the negative in order, by offering it
to God, to turn it into positive love? Have I started to
understand what loving means at all?

In the giving of his presence some of the things God seems
to be saying are:

  I can heal you
  I can bring you to a wholeness where suffering becomes
    part of your glory
  I want to use you to join in Jesus' work of turning what
    is destructive into what is constructive. And there's
    only one way to do that, which is by a wooing,
    seeking love
  I want you to live in increasing fullness
  I want you to receive and offer as I have received and
    offered throughout eternity.

Availability and unavailability

As we respond to God in these things, then we become
more like him. The image of his creative love catches fire
in us. We are all attracted to warmth and we may find
that, as we love God more, so other people gravitate
towards us. They're not always sure what they want and
they couldn't put a name like "God" to their desire but the
"Come" of Jesus is now felt as an attraction towards us.
People have a sixth sense about love. Sooner or later we
know if it's genuine or if a person is really trading off us.

Sometimes learning to love is learning to let go. I remember a story I read not long ago written by a woman whose father was dying. She loved him very much and was sitting by the bed with him through the long hours of pain and laboured breathing. She sat and she sat, and still he didn't die; or rather, couldn't die. She began to sense that in a way she couldn't explain, or didn't want to, she was holding on to him. A friend came to take over the vigil for the night. At first the daughter was reluctant to leave.

"You go and get some sleep," her friend urged. "I'll call you if you're needed."

Some hours later, the friend woke her. "You'd better come now."

The daughter was with her father when he died but, looking back on the experience after some months, she wrote that she felt her absence from the room for a few hours was necessary in order to allow her father to die. Her love was, she felt, expressed by her not being there. The removal of her tenacious presence helped her father finally to ease his grip on Earth.

Sometimes, our unavailability is necessary in order for someone else to hear the voice of God. It doesn't help if we encourage others to rely on us too much. There's an old story which illustrates this. Two men were walking through a dark forest together at night. One of the men held a lantern. The other could see by the light of his friend's lantern. But then they came to a parting of the ways. The man with the lantern continued as before: the other was lost. Our availability can sometimes be used as an excuse for others to walk by a borrowed light. The removal of our availability spurs them on to find the light for themselves.

Any attraction to us will not harm us at all so long, as Jesus put it, "the eye is single". Remaining single-sighted will keep us filled with light. And what is the eye to gaze on so fixedly? On God. If we continue to turn and turn and turn to the Lord then we will not become self-conscious. We unconsciously channel people to God whether his name is mentioned or not. It's only when we're self-conscious that we're tempted to think we're "of help" to others or to see ourselves as a helper.

The person who has learned to love the Lord in stillness looks at God and remains unconcerned with whatever label people try to fix on him. People may flow and people may ebb and the gifts of the Spirit may be used to meet the flows and ebbs of their needs. But in the centre of the currents, the heart remains fixed. There's good advice in the writings of Proverbs, "Guard your heart more than any treasure, for it is the source of all life." (Proverbs 4:23) Sometimes the person who prays is attractive to others and sometimes he isn't. Sometimes he is a helper and sometimes he isn't. Sometimes he's available and sometimes he makes himself unavailable. But his joy doesn't lie in any of these things. His joy lies in the love of God.

> Father, thank you that you are our joy
> Thank you that you always want to give
> much more than we want to receive.

7

CHANGING COURSES

Intercession

Love is a beckoning word. As we allow more of the love of God into our lives we find that, increasingly, we're attracted to others in prayer. No one goes to Heaven alone!

Real attraction offers freedom. That's why I'm suspicious if someone declares, "I love you" and then wants to track down my every move, quizzes me about my conversations and won't let me near anyone else. Sooner or later, I turn round and say, "No. You don't love me. What you call love is just possessiveness." Perhaps when we first pray for others we pray with just such a closed fist. We think we know what's wrong with them or their situation and we tell the Lord everything about it from our point of view. Having done that, we outline what we think should be done to improve matters.

As we sense more of God's presence we become less possessive of our own way of looking at things. We have experienced that God is a mystery. The more we experience, the more we want and the more we suspect there is to want. We are beginning to know that we do not know. Other people are God's image. Other people, we start to sense, are a mystery too. Like us they walk in time with the imprint of eternity. Other people are holy. And they are different from us with a diversity which we now find it easier to accept. As we pray for them, we become less directive.

Perhaps our prayer is more along the lines of taking a person by the hand, in our imagination, and leading him to God. I picture this as God, me and the person, hand in hand, all connected and ever turning towards each other.

Sometimes I literally move my arms and hands in these introductions and remain with hands connected as a physical prayer of intercession.

Another symbol of intercession occurred to me when I was walking through town. The River Stour twists through Canterbury and bridges criss-cross it at regular intervals. One day last summer as I watched crowds of tourists crossing the bridges the somewhat obvious thought flipped into my mind – without these bridges there'd be no connection between the two banks. The bridge provides a way for the traffic to cross. It's the same in prayer. I can stand as a bridge between the love of God and the person for whom I'm praying. Sometimes I actually stand and stretch out my arms in connection. All I am doing is providing a means by which the mercy, love and attraction of God can flow to someone else. There's no need for words. The Spirit, as St. Paul tells us, can interpret for us. All we do is exercise connections. We're starting to understand that everything is connected because nothing exists outside God. So when we pray, we can leave the list of ideas behind and just "be" for the other person before God. Our connections with others are at their strongest when we pray like this for we're in the realms of life where the small talk, the superficial judgments, the excuses and half understandings perceived as complete understanding, drop away. Jesus is always interceding for all of us, and what we do now is to join our little concern to his blazing love. As with people who come to us physically for help, so spiritually we don't turn our eyes from God to them but seek to incorporate them into our gaze.

I've also found that in the silence beyond words, the Lord has asked me to pray for someone. So I start to hold that person before God. The holding might continue on and off all day. Often the preoccupation with another person starts outside prayer, when I'm shopping or baking or during a break at work. Without ceremony, that specific person out of all others (and I might not have been thinking about her for weeks) insinuates herself into my spirit, pulls up a chair and makes herself thoroughly present in a way which nags me to hold her before the Lord. This happened especially vividly some years ago. I hardly knew the person in question and it was only about a week later that I bumped into someone who knew him a lot better than I. "Was anything special happening for Eric last Wednesday?" I asked.

"Oh yes, that was the day of his final interview for theological college. He was feeling really jumpy about it."

"Did he get in?"

"He doesn't know yet. They said they'd let him know in a couple of weeks."

About a month after that I heard he'd been accepted.

There's one friend in particular who I can almost guarantee will sense when I'd be most grateful for a word with her. At times of great stress or tension, the phone rings and I pick it up to the sound of her voice asking, "How are you?" And she's one of those rare people who mean the question and can cope with a truthful answer. I'm so grateful that the Lord slips me in as an irritation under people's spirits from time to time.

Joy and pain

A new sensitivity to others, on the level at which we're all connected in God, can paint broader strokes across our prayer too. There's an old saying, "God whispers to us in our joy but shouts to us in our suffering." We become much more in tune with both the joy and anguish of God and the joy and anguish of the world. The rainbow gladness of the world's joy colours our spirit but the fierce claws of the world's anguish rake and spike us. In his letter to Rome St. Paul advised Christians, "with the joyful be joyful, and mourn with the mourners." Now, sometimes in prayer, this happens without our bidding. But at some deep level of our offering to God we have already given our consent, for the Spirit never forces us.

During one period of silence when I wasn't feeling particularly buoyant in myself, I suddenly felt a bubble of joy form in me, grow and cascade through the prayer. It was as if something of all our happiness, its meetings and weddings, births, families, friendships – all our little, fractured loves, leapt home to the great wholeness of joy in God. Quite suddenly I found myself laughing. It was the laughter of shared companionship; that moment of recognition when, in your happiness, you turn to someone else, hug her and say, "You too?" I remember the words "You too" rippled through the laughter. They symbolised the completeness of sharing and newness that we call joy. It's what we're after in all the weddings and meetings and friendships and births. A current of that wholeness flowed through me for I don't know how many minutes. But it streamed like a foretaste of the wholeness of community in Heaven when we will enjoy each other completely and without end. It also left me with an increased desire to carve out a much greater capacity for the enjoyment of others now. That laughter taught me that it is in an unselfconscious appreciation of others that one of my greatest joys lies. I also saw how very much my own desires interfere with such a richness of living.

Perhaps it is a matter of temperament or perhaps it is a matter of God shouting but I find that more than pitching me into the world's hope, prayer scourges me with the world's sorrow. There's one particular incident which stands for me as a symbol of our horrific carelessness of one another. I saw on a TV news bulletin a short account of a worsening political situation in one of the Third World countries. Reporters and camera crews were scrambling out of the area. Obviously they were using up the last of the film as they went, for they captured what happened to a young American reporter at a check point. Unarmed and trying to leave the country, he was searched briefly by the single army guard on duty and then told to lie face down on the ground. He did this. First the guard kicked him in the thigh. The reporter didn't complain or react. Then the guard drew his pistol and shot the young man in the head. The entire body quivered and jerked in the dust. No words were spoken as commentary but that shot resounds again and again through my prayer.

We may live lives of relative comfort and safety. Many of us have never been to war. But the world God loves is a world of senseless killing, of mass imprisonment, of constant exploitation, of economic wrongs, of rape and violence and tragedies which we could have avoided. But someone somewhere didn't take the trouble to avoid the tragedy, and as a result people die. The lives of those who love them crumble and break up. Such crumbling and break-up agonises and bleeds. And something dies.

The God of peace and wholeness does not cry peace where there is no peace. He takes the world's hurt into himself: it makes imprints in his hands and feet, and it thrusts itself as a spear into his side. He agonises and he bleeds. And he dies. In prayer God sometimes asks us to agonise and bleed a little too. It's difficult work but in it we are joining ourselves to the ever-renewed reconciling of the world to God which is Jesus' work of prayer. We may find that, at times, our sense of the presence of God is fogged in an appalling greyness of distress and confusion and loss as we take on board something of a more general ache and brokenness.

As with all intercession, we take on board only to pour into God. If you are imaginative or relatively thin-skinned it is rather easy to get swamped by any tapping into sorrow. This is no help to the world at all. You don't rescue a drowning man by feeling such compassion for him that you drown yourself. You haven't altered his situation for the better at all and so you can hardly expect him to be grateful for your *beau geste*. Through the pain and tears it is important continually to channel the sorrow to God. In this prayer we are again standing like a bridge. Standing in such conditions is far from easy. If you look at the passage in the letter to the Ephesians which describes spiritual warfare, you'll find instructions to put on God's armour. And the reason for such arms? So that you can stand. This standing is so important that it is to continue when every task is completed. The standing is the whole reason for all the armour in the first place. I find I can do this more easily by repeating a simple phrase such as

"Lord have mercy" or by saying the "Our Father" very slowly and reflectively through the pain. You may even just hold a cross or a rose for the world as a way of prayer.

I don't like such prayer. It's extremely uncomfortable and I often try to dodge it. The most effective defence in my retreat from the pain of the world is the pleasant cushioning of everyday routines. Then, planning the week's menus anaesthetises concern for political prisoners in other countries and my fervour for the January sales drowns out the cries of the starving. Such a diminishing of the world to the size of my greed is a sure measure of my failure to respond to God. Often I grow weak at the knees, and my standing topples over into the slump of lazy sitting. The only remedy then is to say sorry to the Lord and to trust him to hoist me to my feet again. God's arms are very strong and very patient.

Prayer and powers

God's creation is much bigger than what we can see of it. Not only does it include galaxies and systems whose distance we can hardly calculate but it includes the unseen powers; forces inside us and forces outside. In prayer some people enter into these different realms and experience something of their power.

In the nineteenth century a parish priest of an obscure area of France called Ars was famous for his spiritual perception. So discerning was he that people queued up day and night to speak with him. For years his ministry was mainly that of such counselling. At the end of long hours of listening to others he'd retire to his room to pray and then to snatch a little sleep. Sometimes his rest was punctuated by disturbance. At times the disturbance was quite violent, wrecking his sleep and moving furniture about the room. After each particularly violent episode, the parish priest chuckled, "We'll catch a big fish in the net tomorrow." And the next day either an especially hardened person arrived wanting his help or an unusually large number of pilgrims and penitents came to his door.

He understood that, although God is drawing everything to himself, there are forces and powers which resist such attraction. Where the Spirit of God is working most strongly, there too resistance to the Spirit will show itself most strongly.

I have only rarely encountered such disturbance in prayer. But when it happens every hair on my body prickles, I sense the cold and my entire system races to "red alert". I'm not very practised at putting my fear into God and can usually be found fleeing the house in order to get amongst people and "normality". But those with more spiritual stability than I, those whose knees don't buckle, have sometimes fought frequent battles against obvious evil. I know that this is a facet of prayer that is given to and accepted by some but, as I have such limited experience of it, I feel I shouldn't try to write any more about it at present.

Alienation

There's one form of suffering in the world which is always present but which, in the last hundred years or so, has been named far more than it was before. This is the suffering of alienation and its resultant sense of meaninglessness.

Modern literature gives us many examples of "the outsider", the person who cannot feel part of anything or connected with anyone. The need to belong is one aspect of God's image in us. God the Father, Son and Spirit all belong to one another and this characteristic, given to us, sends us out again and again looking for somewhere or someone to whom we matter. Failure to find a niche for ourselves is the ushering in of that terrible isolation we call Hell. Hell is being trapped behind the iron bars of myself.

A programme on TV recently showed several people who'd been bereaved. One young woman, left a widow very suddenly as a result of an accident, talked about bringing up her three small daughters. She then went on to speak of one of the profound effects of her husband's death on her. "It was as if I died too. All that I was to this person, all my specialness, was gone. I have to create a new personality for myself now."

We need to be special to someone. The more people we feel special to, the more our sense of value increases. That's why some of us who are mothers have such a hard time letting our older children go. We say that old habits die hard and that once a parent, always a parent! So we worry and fret over them, and they fight us off to gain their independence. Are we really worrying over our children? Or are we worrying over ourselves? I, who have been so long a mother, who am I when my child has gone? It's the same for a lot of us regarding jobs or any other roles we fulfil. We're right. Old habits die very hard, and the habit of defining ourselves in terms of very obvious indispensability is just one of them. We all have in us the terror of failing to connect. It's this terror that makes us cling to whatever obvious connections we have with all the desperation of a drowning man clinging to his piece of splintering driftwood.

As we experience something of the love of God, so we begin to ease away from possessiveness in our contacts. We fear alienation less, and so we can let others "be" more. We don't have to grasp and to cling. We start to experience the love of God for us. I know that I am special because I am special to God. I was chosen for love before the world began. I am important because God loves me, and the universe would be a poorer place if I had not been born. Do you believe that? If you find your importance to God difficult to accept, then imagine the Lord standing near you. Look at him. He is already looking at you. His eyes are full of kindness and enjoyment of you. Now he is speaking to you; he is calling you by special names. You are his Child, his Chosen One, his Delight. Now think of other names the Lord calls his people in the Bible. You are God's present to himself.

Once we experience our value to God then we are thrilled when other people love us too. But others come and others go, and we start to sense that all love is an offshoot of the love of God. The love of God will not run out and so we begin to trust the Lord enough to allow change to happen, to move and to let go.

Then, just as we move into the joy of so much shared love, we hit the brick wall of alienation again. But this time the bricks are not made of our own alienation but of a little of all the remaining unconnectedness in the universe. The Holy Spirit is inviting us to link the world's brokenness to God's wholeness. So we stand in the middle of anxiety or darkness and, in prayer – perhaps in silence or in the speaking of some words of scripture – gently draw that aloneness into the community of God. Such aloneness is far deeper than the passing boredom of the continually active who are temporarily deprived of something to do. It is an aloneness which shrivels the spirit with its chill and fear. Its only offspring is meaninglessness. As love is its own meaning, so the absence of love ushers in the absence of meaning. The more we fail to connect, the more we experience loss of meaning. That's why some of us who may even have studied theology can be plagued by depression and the sense that nothing matters. Intellectually we may know a great deal more than others about God's plans for the universe and about meaning given through Jesus Christ. But thinking cannot make it so. Unless we remain still enough to allow the love of God to expel our isolation and well up in us, our intellectual grasp will turn out to be a fist clutched tight round a handful of straw. Martin Luther was at times prey to just such attacks of meaninglessness. During one particularly dark period his wife, Catherine, arrived downstairs for breakfast dressed in the black of deep mourning.

"Why are you wearing that?" her husband asked.

"Because God is dead," she replied.

It did the trick. Martin Luther turned to worship once more and slowly discovered his God to be alive.

Fear

St. John in his first letter tells us that, "perfect love banishes fear". Sometimes, being used as a link between the world's fear and the love of God leads us to discover fears in ourselves which, to date, we'd managed to keep well hidden.

God's love has poured healing into old wounds or has taken up our suffering into something of his wholeness, and now we're ready to enter a further stage of the journey. We may find we are called to meet not just our hurts of the past but our fears of the future. For some the future still shines bright with easy hopes. Big decisions about job and marriage lie in front of them. But for a lot of us the time of easy hopes is past. We may have learned to accept loss in our past but can we face the fear of loss in the future? It's not just the obvious losses like bereavement or retirement (when we lose our quantifiable usefulness, status and something to do) but it's the loss of our competence.

Earlier in our lives we could chat about creativity and bask in the warmth of that hope. But later all that seems open is a lessening; a lessening in value to society, in physical strength and attractiveness, usefulness at home, ability to think and act. Old age may lurk ahead like a robbery taking much that we recognise of value. Perhaps your fear is not of old age but of some hideous accident resulting in helplessness and deformity. Only you know what your fears are. They may still lie in that strange, eerie territory named alienation. Then, what we fear most about the future is that, whatever it's like, it won't deliver any comfort: that somehow, whatever changes come will be loss and theft of our value.

On the other hand whatever we have now, in a real sense, crowds out our ability to receive other gifts. Try this. Stop reading and close this book. Hold it in your hand. That's fine. You've got a book but now you've no room for anything else.

In the same way our loss of what we are now may, in

God's love, make room for another gift. What we think we dread may turn out to be an invitation of joy. But how can I be reconciled to my fear? How can I let God turn my fear into joy? May I suggest one or two imaginative exercises through which the Holy Spirit can lead us into peace?

In the Book of Revelation, John describes the call of Jesus to his people as an invitation to celebrate at a great feast. In your spirit, say "Yes" to the invitation. Look at the tables laden with good things. Smell the warmth. Gaze round at the other guests, at their happy faces. See, they're beckoning you to come closer. Now you catch sight of Jesus. He's got both arms open wide pleading with you to come to him. You hurry in response. And you bring everything that you know about yourself with you. Your fear, too, is a welcome guest. Your as yet unconscious anxieties are invited. And so, too, is your death. Bring them to the welcome of Christ and let him feed them with his love. Recognise their presence and lead them all to the welcome God gives. Let your fears respond in their own time. Some may feast on love immediately and be turned to joy. Others may need to be taken to the banquet for several years before they are really convinced of their welcome.

The bread and wine of communion are part of Jesus' feast on earth. You may like to invite your anxieties, fears and compulsions to that meal too.

There's another picture the Bible offers us, and that's the waters of baptism. This time, in your imagination, go to the water's edge and hold out your hands. Don't move until everything that frightens you has clasped onto your hands. Let them gather round. Let them bring your death to join them. Jesus is standing on the bank with you. Turn to him now. He blesses you and his blessing takes in everything which your hands are holding. Then lead all of you, all that string of what you find difficult, down into the water. Let the waters come up over you. Go down gradually, gently, step by step. The bank is firm and the descent is not difficult. Allow the water to close over your head. Your eyes are open and you can tell that you are on the

bottom now. There is nothing visible of you from above.
You have gone down as far as you can and you are out of
anyone else's sight. But you do not lose confidence. Jesus
has blessed you. Jesus has desired this for you.

Now look ahead. You can see Jesus again. He, too, is in
the water and you are not alone. He will lead you to
resurrection out of the water from this, your lowest point.
The timing will be right for the timing will be his. He has
you by the hand.

You may just like to bring your fears to Jesus for him to
pour the oil of his healing over them. Again, walk to Jesus
with your fears. He is welcoming you. He holds a bottle in
his hand. As you stand in front of him, he pours some of the
contents of the bottle over your head. The perfume is
wonderful. The scent of the oil fills your nostrils with its
sweetness. Some of the balm flows over your fears. Let
them enjoy it too.

Now, spend a few minutes thanking the Lord that your
fear is surrounded by his love; nothing about you is outside
his love.

Deeper repentance

Our growing connections with the rest of God's world are
accompanied by a growing connection within ourselves.
As part of God's work in us we may find he sends us back
over our lives in prayer once more. This time the journey is
not towards the healing of past hurts but towards the
healing of a deeper repentance. Incidents which we
haven't thought about for years suddenly flash, with all
the vividness of Technicolor, on to the screen of our
memory. Why is this?

God does not exist in time. Time only exists in God. It is
part of creation and, like everything else, lives and moves
in its creator. When we allow God to come to us in prayer
then he takes our life in time up into the perspective
of eternity. It's all a bit like puzzles you sometimes see
on TV. First the camera shows something we can't dis-
tinguish and a voice tells us this is part of a bigger object.

We have to try to guess what the bigger object is from that little part. Then the camera moves back a pace or two and we can see more. Can we guess now? And so on until the whole object is revealed. Sin, like a strand of mistletoe, may have lodged itself in a crevice in our past. From that point it sucks and drains much of the sap of the rest of our life. Past sin, which we may have forgotten about, can be spoiling our present. As our time is taken up into the viewpoint of eternity, the Holy Spirit directs the eye of our spirit to zoom in over past events which have, so far, lain out of focus in the shadows. We begin to understand how the sin in one part of our life in the past is connected to the larger picture as we know it to date. Once the sin comes to light, then all that we have to do is to ask God's forgiveness.

When this first happened to me I had quite a large problem in accepting forgiveness. Maybe it's because, for us, the past feels so fixed and unalterable. But our view of time is not God's and he is not confined as we so often are. Because of my recoil from old sins which had blighted my life down the years, I felt the need of some concrete assurance of my forgiveness. When I was walking by the river, it struck me that I could pick up some pebbles. So I did. Each pebble represented one of my old sins which had come to light. One by one I threw them into the water and watched with pleasure as they vanished from sight. The waters of God's love can wash away all my unlove.

If feelings of guilt or inadequacy remain then it is a good idea to take the advice of St. Paul. He told the early Christians to ". . . give thanks every day for everything to our God and Father." (Ephesians 5:20) It seems strange but nothing about us is or has been outside God's love. All our life, from birth and from the time before we responded to God's love, is held in God. In a way we often don't understand, everything (and that must include what we would judge as unhelpful) works for good for the lovers of God. If God does not judge us, who are we to judge ourselves?

When we come closer to God, we start to understand

why it is that some of the people we would think of as the
greatest saints felt themselves to be full of sin. In chapter
six of his book, Isaiah describes the Lord of his vision as
"high and exalted". His response is to cry out, "Woe is me! I
am lost, for I am a man of unclean lips." The closer we are
drawn by the wholeness of God, the greater is our horror at
our own fracture and destruction. We can only lie flat on
our faces in awe. But the Lord picks us up, caresses us,
cleanses us and accepts us. Our love leaps in response.
This gratitude is the small, fragile seed from which humility will grow. From humility springs freedom, for freedom
is the place where you find you have nothing to lose. So,
those who see their sins by the light of the Holy Spirit are
characterised both by reverence for God and a kind of holy
levity which doesn't take itself too seriously. Heaven is
reserved for the joyful.

Once we have entered into repentance for our own past,
the Lord may lead us to repent for the past of our family or
friends, or for wider circles such as our city or our nation.
Then, in prayer, we stand as a bridge over which a dark
past can be drawn into the marvellous light of God's
ever-present where it is cleansed and made whole. When
we do this we are journeying, in a small way, as Jesus
journeyed after his death. In the Creed we express this as
"he descended into hell", and we mean he journeyed into
the land of the dead. This, by its very nature, is the land of
the past. (Isn't the past always another country?) In this
way, Jesus brought the dead past into the living present of
God.

Gradually, I am beginning to see that all my prayer for
others is only a tiny participation in Jesus' continuing
prayer for all of us in all ages. We can make no journey
where he has not gone before, and there is nothing in us or
in the old and spiteful world that he has not experienced
and accepted and is longing to heal. All our prayer is a
journey within the heart of Jesus.

Concern for the world

Perhaps our understanding of wholeness has expanded
a little too. It's no longer so small and self-protecting,
excluding everything which hurts it. It has grown to
include pain and hurt and tension. Love, we begin to see,
is, in a very vital sense, suffering. The sword is piercing
our heart also. Strangely, the peace that God gives is
beginning to feel rather disturbing at times. The concerns
of the Lord Jesus are speaking to us and, as scripture
warns, ". . . the word of God is alive and active. It cuts more
keenly than any two-edged sword, piercing as far as the
place where life and spirit, joints and marrow, divide. It
sifts the purposes and thoughts of the heart. There is
nothing in creation that can hide from him; everything
lies naked and exposed . . ." (Hebrews 4:12–13)

This, too, is part of the abundance of life that Jesus wants
for us. Life is not all a bed of roses and, as we allow God to
move in us, so he brings life with him. He is the life and
nothing can hide from him. Wherever we journey, we
cannot journey beyond Jesus Christ. He has always gone
farther than we can. By identifying with the sins of
everyone when he was on the cross, he was thrust as far as
anyone can ever go from God. Because of this it is difficult
to enter into the work of prayer and to remain naïve for
long. God's love is for the here and now in its aspects that
terrify as well as those that please. He will protect our
purity. To be pure is to keep the eye single: it is not to close
it. So God moves us from naïvity to purity. He beckons us
to see and he gives us the strength to cope with what we
see. Those who pray grow increasingly unshockable.

Jesus told us that God is good. In fact, he said, "No one is
good except God alone." (Luke 18:19) God's goodness, as
we have seen, is not an overlooking of evil, nor is it
ignorance of evil but it is something very alive and purposeful. God's goodness always journeys out to overcome
evil. What has turned destructive he seeks to make constructive. God creates and re-creates: he restores and woos
and empowers. And he never gives up. His goodness is not

an absence of badness but it is like a fire, a living, moving thing in itself. It seems that it is evil which is dead, in a sense a sort of non-goodness; something which should have been filled with goodness and wasn't.

God's goodness doesn't bring him the relaxation of complacency. It brings him the desire to give up his fullness and, in his burning love, to enter the terrible emptiness of his fallen creation. God's goodness results in Jesus. It gets its hands very dirty indeed.

Sometimes Jesus' goodness takes strange forms. In its positive fight against the emptiness, it calls people "whited sepulchres" and it hurls money changers and their tables out of the temple. It upsets the religious status quo. It is neither very cosy nor very safe. It demands only the best of its friends. Do you remember the time when Peter urged Jesus not to go to Jerusalem because he was frightened for him? Jesus replied, "Get behind me, Satan." It was not always easy being one of Jesus' friends. This goodness felt attraction for a young man who wished to follow the teaching, and then imposed a condition which made it impossible for the young man to follow. "Come," said Jesus. But, "Give your riches to the poor – sell what you have – follow me." This is, at times, a strange, austere and angry goodness. If we are afraid of anger, never feel it or, if we feel it, smother our reaction immediately, then we are possibly cutting ourselves off in some way from the goodness of God.

As we come to the God of Justice in prayer, our world grows bigger, and our happy, insulated complacency is blown from us. We can no longer be bounded by our own comforts. The "I'm all right, Jack" attitude slips through our fingers, and all our scrabbling cannot recapture it. In its place, we are invaded by a growing horror at the injustices of our world. We may even feel accused by the Spirit when we discover that some of the wealthier economic systems thrive at the cost of the poorer elements in their own society. They may also grow fat on exploitation of societies on the other side of the world.

The Spirit may kindle something of the anger of the

prophets in us, especially against those who use religion as a guard over their eyes so that they may not see what the world is like. Equally, they may teach that God has nothing to do with all of society: in doing this, they hedge him into a corner where he is rendered impotent by religious platitudes and piety.

It was against just such a religion that exploited the world or ignored the wider issues of society, being content to grow fat on pickings rather than to strive to bring God's justice to all people, that the prophet Amos spoke. His words flay those who, down the centuries, exploit the poor and the underprivileged on the one hand (or make no protest when their governments do so) and yet are full of religious talk and turn up at every religious meeting, on the other hand. To act in this way is blasphemy for it is to worship a God who is not there. Perhaps we need to listen to Amos once more:

> Fools who long for the day of the Lord,
> What will the day of the Lord mean to you?
> It will be darkness not light.
> It will be as when a man runs from a lion,
> and a bear meets him,
> or turns into a house and leans his hand on the wall,
> and a snake bites him.
> The day of the Lord is indeed darkness, not light,
> a day of gloom with no dawn.
>
> (Amos 5:18–20)

The Lord continues to speak against such false religion:

> I hate, I spurn your pilgrim-feasts;
> I will not delight in your sacred ceremonies.
> When you present your sacrifices and offerings
> I will not accept them . . .
> Spare me the sound of your songs . . .
>
> (Amos 5:21–22)

There have been many voices since Amos fell silent. One of the latest belonged to a South American church leader who questioned his rich government's neglect of the suffering and rights of the poor. He too fell silent, shot at the altar of his church during a service.

Brother Jesus, let me not think I can turn from my
    brothers to you
Father God, forgive me my laziness and blindness
Spirit of God, kindle in me a desire for your goodness.
Open my eyes, Lord, make me see.

8

STRUGGLING, GROWING

Let's hold up that diamond of the sense of the presence of God again. Through all the fullness and the joy, the silence whispered two more questions:

1) Doesn't love like this kill you in the end?
2) How can all not be brought to completion?

The rest of this book will be an attempt to explore these questions.

Doesn't love like this kill you in the end?

If we look at the life and ministry of Jesus, the answer seems to be "Yes". And, in his case, the death was of a young man in his prime, by means of a particularly painful and public execution. The early Church drew strength from the blood of the martyrs and, throughout the ages, Christians have died for the faith. I once heard that the twentieth century has produced more martyrs than all the previous centuries put together.

But Jesus talked about another sort of death and he expressed himself in the strange language of paradox, which is so suitable for talking about the deepest experiences. He likened an individual life to a grain of wheat, and drawing on his knowledge of how they did things in the fields around him, remarked, ". . . a grain of wheat remains a solitary grain unless it falls into the ground and dies; but if it dies, it bears a rich harvest." (John 12:24) He spoke again on the same theme, more directly this time, in Luke 9:23–26, "If anyone wishes to be a follower of mine, he must leave self behind; day after day he must take up his cross, and come with me. Whoever cares for his own safety is lost: but if a man will let himself be lost for my sake, that man is safe. What will a man gain by winning the whole world, at the cost of his true self?"

Such language is a wine of heady words. What can it mean? There's talk of death in life, and Jesus speaks of two selves; a false self and a true one. How can one fall to the ground to die? And does the underground grain have the foggiest idea that, if it stays there long enough, it'll grow into a harvest? It all sounds rather risky and very unattractive. The letters of the apostles don't offer us much of an escape from this either. We read in Colossians 3:3, ". . . you died; and now your life lies hidden with Christ in God." This seems to take us one step further: not only are we told we just die, but we now hear we have died!

You have probably already discovered that to pray is to change. It is to grow into the ability to listen and to look. It is also to get to know yourself. It is not possible to get to know God better without learning something more about yourself. This is because God is everywhere; inside us as well as around us. We change by making connections. We also change by recognising connections. We travel back into the past and we put our future into God. We build bridges to other people. We start to live in a larger world which is, at once, more joyful and more demanding. We notice that little, everyday things are full of wonder. All this change has been both a deepening and an expanding. It may have brought pain but that pain has been part of an enlarging whole. So far, we have not grown less, we have grown bigger. Everything is ours because we are Christ's and Christ is God's.

Suddenly we hear different words. We hear that to pray is to die; not the grand gesture of a death by martyrdom but a dying that is private and unnoticed by those around us. To pray, we hear, is to enter into a living death. That doesn't sound at all delightful. In fact it sounds frightening because death is the unknown and we have no experience of that.

"How can love kill us?" we ask. Love is what has brought

us to life. We love God because he first loved us. We often say that all the world loves a lover. But isn't that because a lover loves all the world? Connections again, and the spark of the Holy Spirit leading us into joy.

But, if we think again, we remember that to love is to give. The cry of love is a cry of offering, "Have what you like. All I have is yours." I remember reading a story which was full of love's offering.

There was a young married couple who loved each other very much. They were poor but that didn't seem to matter too much. Except that he was an artist and poverty meant he had to paint what he could sell rather than what he wanted to paint. It seemed out of the question but, if he could only afford to buy some much finer, very expensive brushes, he felt sure he could put on canvas the pictures which lived so vividly in his imagination. The money wasn't there. Day after day he painted what didn't really interest him in order to sell enough work to pay their rent and buy some food. There was nothing left over for new clothes or meals out or holidays. Gradually, he put a little by towards the good quality brushes but nowhere near enough. He lived with the fear that if he didn't get sufficient together soon, he'd lose the vision from his mind completely. And that seemed to open up a future of despair. He didn't share much of this with his young wife in case it depressed her too. But she loved him and, by sensing his moods, realised what was wrong.

This wife was beautiful, and the most beautiful thing about her was her hair. She didn't moan or complain about the shortage of money and she did her best to eke out what food they had. She didn't even mind the dull routine of the days in their two rooms, or never having a new dress. Apart from the love of her husband, which she had already got, there was just one thing she wanted. Her long, thick hair streamed down her back the colour of russet apples and with a sheen like theirs too. In one of the jeweller's shops where they wandered during the soft, autumn evenings, she'd seen a tortoiseshell comb that would look magnificent holding up the weight of her hair. It wasn't terribly expensive but it was more than they could afford. Besides which, what of his new brushes? She didn't talk about it to her husband. But sometimes in an afternoon, she'd sneak out of the house to press her nose against the jeweller's shop window and, once or twice, when they wandered in the area together, her gaze strayed to it again. She pulled herself away quickly. Her husband mustn't know of her longing.

Christmas approached. What to buy her? What to give him? In the country where they lived, Christmas gifts were exchanged on Christmas Eve.

That Christmas Eve she stole out earlier than usual in the afternoon. Her lips were pressed together in a thin, purposeful line that drove all the colour from them, and she wore her largest bonnet which partially screened her paler than normal face. Unknown to her, once she'd left the house, her husband too stopped work, wiped clean his cheap brushes and, with a little sigh, covered the "chocolate box" painting of the day.

She arrived home at five o'clock and was just about to go into their rooms when he, too, ran up to the door. They went inside.

"Shall we exchange presents straight away?" he suggested.

"All right."

He held out a small, beautifully wrapped package to her. "Go on. Undo it," he urged. With fingers a little slow from the cold, she managed to untie the red ribbon. The paper fell apart.

"Oh, it's lovely!" she exclaimed. She picked up the tortoiseshell comb she'd wanted for so long.

"Here. This is for you." She held out a long, thin parcel to her husband.

Eagerly, he broke into it. He gasped and then held two beautiful, fine brushes to the light. The individual hairs glowed softly. "But these are far more expensive than I could have got," he muttered.

"Yes. And you bought the comb instead," she reminded him gently.

"Let me see it in your hair."

Slowly, very slowly, she untied the ribbon of her bonnet. After a moment's hesitation, breathed on a sigh, she took off the hat.

"What have you done to all your lovely hair?" her husband cried.

"I found a place where they gave me a good price for it. It'll make a couple of wigs, they said. It was the only way I could think of to get the brushes."

By the time her hair had grown long enough for her to wear the tortoiseshell comb, he'd sold enough of the "chocolate box" pictures to buy the pigment he needed for use with the fine brushes.

For that young couple, love meant offering, and offering resulted in the death of longing and vision. Neither of them could have known that both longing and vision would return as gift.

The thin-lipped, hard and exacting deaths they experienced were a result of choice. Each chose the other rather than himself. Love led them to choice, and choosing led them to more love. Jesus, too, mentioned choice. It's clear in his question, "What will a man gain by winning the whole world, at the cost of his true self?" This tells us that there's a true self and a false self. There comes a time when the Holy Spirit leads us to a deepening awareness both of our true and our false selves.

Conflict

The journey of prayer starts as a discovery of the beginnings of the true self; that self which is made to connect; that self which celebrates others and itself; that self which seeks to become larger and more sympathetic. Its motto is "Love makes the world go round." So far, we've journeyed away from our false self. The false self is the self which cuts itself off and views other people with wariness; the false self celebrates at the expense of others; the false self is very small indeed. It's as small as its own outlook and interest. But it's terrified that other selves might be bigger. Its motto is 'I'll make the world go round at my pace and in my way."

The Holy Spirit has been leading us gently towards God which means we've recognised something of our true self when suddenly we're pulled up short. The false self, that old, screaming "I" is yanking on the other end of the rope. We're reminded again that Jesus said following him is a daily choice.

How do we experience these tugs of the "I" which are trying to pull us back from God? For each of us they'll take a different form. No one, except God, knows your own particular circumstances and relationships better than you do. However, there are some pulls that a lot of us experience at one time or another. All of them are the tugs of "I" away from the place where a new spirit can be born in us. We're in a life and death struggle, and our own life is fighting for all its worth to keep itself alive.

We do not become aware that there's any struggle until we've journeyed some way towards love. There is no need for a struggle when the battle is completely one-sided. Those who don't want God don't enter such a battle, and for those who possess God in Heaven the battle is over. The rest of us are left, gradually becoming aware that we are living in the divided territory of invitation, choice and compulsion.

The Psalmist declares, ". . . in thy light we are bathed in light." (Psalm 36:9) It is because we are bathed in God's light that we start to see some of our own darkness that we'd not been aware of before. After all, you don't realise just how gloomy the room's become until someone switches on the light. So the discomfort, which is the beginning of our recognition of the dark in us, comes as a direct result of experiencing something of the light of the Holy Spirit leading us further towards God. We are being drawn by God's life towards death and, at times, everything in us revolts against such a letting go that may leave us with nothing we recognise of ourselves. But we have offered and now God is taking us at our word. We're left wondering what we have let ourselves in for.

But we have been warned. Jesus told two stories about the cost of following him. You can find them in Luke 14:28–33. Jesus asks us, "Would any of you think of building a tower without first sitting down and calculating the cost, to see whether you could afford to finish it?" Or again, he wonders which king goes to battle without first totting up the numbers in his army and weighing these against the opposition. The grace of God cannot be estimated; it is free and total. This means that also, at some stage, I will have to consider, is my response free and total?

The answer, in my case, was a sad "No". So all my defence mechanisms flashed onto red alert as I was plummeted into more self-knowledge than before. Deep within me lay the old belief that possession is nine-tenths of the law, and I wanted to fight against losing my possessions. I wanted to hang on to old certainties when they seemed threatened. I wanted to retreat into conformity and intellectual certainty. It all seems so much easier than creativity and trust. But Jesus said that a person's value does not lie in what he possesses and that includes his intellectual possessions. When some of the neat formulas began to fail, I was faced with a choice. Do I accept the passion of doubt as part of the passion of faith? Or do I retreat into a facade of belief – the sort of creed that allows no loopholes anywhere? I once heard of a preacher, preparing his sermon for Sunday. He wanted to make a point but wasn't sure of his ground. He pencilled into the margin of his notes, "Not clear. Bang on pulpit here." We've probably all come across people whose protestation of belief is so bullyingly loud that we wonder what they're afraid of. Doubt which we exclude often takes its revenge by shouting a noisy, ungenerous certainty to the world. It bangs people over the head with its clamour about God but isn't able to listen or receive.

In prayer I discovered that God led me into knowledge through love. Can I not trust him to be sure that the same love will help me to talk about my experience of him? Can I not learn to keep silent about those things I haven't yet experienced? Love has led me, love can be a girding under my ignorance. Jesus was not afraid to be silent about things he didn't know. He said that only his Father knew when he would come again.

We know through love. We can only love if we are also capable of hate. To love is to live a life of continual choice. This is not the way of respectability. Often our respectability is a cloak to hide our indifference just as our conformity masks our fear. Once love leaves the house of our lives, we try to fill the empty, echoing rooms with tattered drapery of habit. Perhaps this is why Jesus was attracted to those who knew they were sinners. In them passion was alive and well and responding. So a tax collector becomes a disciple, a prostitute is forgiven and a thief is promised Paradise. Jesus loved sinners so much that he even elevated the respectable to their ranks.

As our respectability fades under God's love so we can start to experience emotions which tear us apart and frighten us. Before we began to pray our lives were neat, like well-clipped suburban gardens. Now, although we look the same to everyone else, we feel much more as if we're living in a jungle of dark and towering trees, choking creepers and carnivorous plants. And we no longer want to explore this new territory. Gone are the order and manageable foliage. In their place this new, much vaster, untamed space terrifies us. We feel the sun should have brought out more pansies bobbing in neat borders, not the thorns and thistles and choking weeds that are now threatening us.

Anger

Not long ago I met a lady, named Judith, who admitted her terror. She said that once, when she was five, her mother had taken some of her sweets away. She couldn't quite remember why but thought she'd probably been eating them when she shouldn't – or some other five-year-olds misdemeanour. She said that, at the moment when her mother's hand came towards her, like a claw, to rake in the sweets, she hated her. She felt such an impotent anger raging in her that if she'd had a gun or a knife, she'd have killed her mother. All this hardly showed on her face but her small body trembled down to her toes. Her mother hadn't a clue about the fire of anger burning her daughter but the little girl was so afraid of what she wanted to do, that she vowed she'd never feel so cross again. "And I didn't," she complained to me, "until I started to pray. Up until then it was all under control. I didn't feel any rage, ever. I didn't feel much else either . . ." She tailed off.

"And now?"

"It's terrible. The anger's back and lots else. I don't know where I am. I think I'd better stop praying."

"Why?" I asked.

"Because I'm scared I'll go out of control again."

There's no one with such rigid control as the dead! Once we repress a response, we die a little. The more we repress, the more we kill ourselves.

Judith and I looked up what Jesus had to say about anger. He described it in much the terms she'd experienced the emotion. We read in Matthew that Jesus said, "Do not commit murder; anyone who commits murder must be brought to judgment." He follows it immediately with, "But what I tell you is this: anyone who nurses anger against his brother must be brought to judgment." (Matthew 5:21–22) So we are right to fear our anger, or our lingering anger.

Judith, just as I had, found release in the discovery that there is nothing, absolutely nothing, however fearful, that she can feel, that God in Jesus doesn't know about. What's more, he can handle it. We cannot fall through the net of God's mercy.

Once we accept this, we can bear God's light on our dark. We no longer have to push the dark down to a place where we don't look at it. Darkness which is not brought into the light grows in us like a pernicious plant, shooting out tendrils of poison into our lives. Until we allow God's Spirit to lead us to the roots of the plant, we are powerless to prevent the numbing stings and rashes of the venom. We cut off parts of ourselves and walk round with our capacity for love stunted and deformed. Part of God's warming us to life is the painful process of learning to use long-dead, long-cramped aspects of our personality. And that can cause us agony at first. We all know how excruciating even a slight attack of pins and needles is.

Judith was still worried. "But I'm frightened where my anger will go."

"What's the worst place it could go?" I asked.

After a long pause, she whispered, "I suppose, on God. And that's terrible. Because then it's bound to be wrong, isn't it? You can't be angry with God."

"Isn't that what the crucifixion's about?"

We explored together something of what God had done in Jesus during his time on the cross. Jesus had been accused and condemned totally unjustly. On the cross he accepted all this injustice. His acceptance wasn't a passive letting it happen; it was an active "Yes" to the terrible process. Jesus deliberately mounted the cross in full agreement with what would happen. He stretched his arms wide to embrace the rejection. God in Jesus has already taken any unjust anger or petulance or hate that we can throw at him. It cannot harm him. God in Jesus has already said "Yes" to all our negatives and is longing to turn them into positives. Perhaps all our negatives are, in fact, only positives which we haven't started to recognise yet. It's a bit like training a puppy. You could never encourage a puppy towards obedience, good sense and fun unless it had the energy for these things in the first place. Unfortunately, until it's harnessed, this energy demonstrates itself in chewing your best arm chairs, wetting the carpet and jumping up on all visitors. But it's the same energy!

Whatever we throw at God, he can catch and cherish and reform into something positive.

"But why am I feeling like this now?"

We only feel what we dare to feel. As a five year old, Judith had shut down on her anger and, with it, had shut down on some of her capacity for love. Her life was governed by fear. When God's love started to warm and touch her, it wanted to woo her away from that fear. Love has already begun its work. This means that Judith is troubled by what she doesn't like in herself. It also means she is worried that she can't handle it.

We can only admit to what is not pleasant in us to the extent that we feel accepted. What we fear above everything is rejection; that terrible "Go away from me; I never knew you", whether the words slay us from the mouth of God or from the mouths of family and friends. God does not only say to us, "Come" but he encourages us with, "Stay". As I accept and respond to the encouragement, so a little more of the unacceptable me escapes the vigilant, policing respectability. Perhaps this is another reason why the greatest saints feel themselves to be dark sinners. Literally, they could afford to. They have enough love to squander some on their unpleasantness. They have learned to look at, accept and embrace what is dark in themselves. Because of this, they are no longer afraid. "There is no room for fear in love," St. John tells us. (1 John 4:18) The cry of the saints is, "I am so loved!" Because of this, they respond, "Lord, I am not worthy."

All our looking at our darkness is nothing new to God. He has been there before us. He already knows us through and through. As the Psalmist says, ". . . if I make my bed in Sheol, again I find thee." (Psalm 139:8) We all have a little hell within us; God sees it already; God loves it. Through our response to him in love, he wants to lead us by his Spirit into the dark in ourselves to draw it into his marvellous light.

A few weeks later, Judith and I chatted again over coffee. "The funny thing is," she reflected, "all that anger I was so terrified of isn't half as frightening as I thought. Once I let it get out a little, it rather fizzled away. I suppose it's a bit like the build-up in a volcano. If the top rock holds all the lava in, there's got to be a massive explosion but if there are vent holes everywhere, then the steam escapes before too much damage is done."

Resentment

Sometimes a stream of anger cools into the hard rock of resentment. The harder the rock, the more difficult to shift it. If I sense resentment building its layers in me, I first of all try to go over whatever I'm resentful about from the point of view of the other person. If my hardness persists then, in my imagination, I look at my resentment and then I look at Jesus on the cross. I do this two or three times and then leave the exercise. Next time in prayer I repeat the looking. Gradually, the resentment shrivels into the tiny dead thing it is, whilst its energy is taken up into the mercy of God. As the resentment dies, my freedom is reborn.

Keeping it safe

Because coming to life can be so painful, I'm quite slow to respond to the Holy Spirit in some areas of my personality, preferring to keep them lifeless and so, controlled. In America it's now possible to have your beloved pet stuffed when it dies. The taxidermist takes the body, cleans it out and arranges your pet in the pose of your choice. Apparently prices vary according to pose. It's cheaper to have a dog sitting down than doing one of its party tricks begging for titbits, balanced on its hind legs.

Once you get your pet back you can arrange it in its customary corner of the house, perhaps in front of the fire. There it will remain with every semblance of life except response. You can kick it, pour coffee over it, cuddle it, and it'll still fix you with the same stare. Its coat will remain bright and burnished. Everything will be as it should be except for that vital difference we call being alive. Unfortunately, because it's not alive, it could get a bad attack of the moth or mildew.

Perhaps it's wiser even with pets, to follow Jesus' advice, "Let the dead bury the dead."

I, for one, don't always follow that advice. I've got lots of my personality carefully groomed and arranged, sitting

neatly in front of the fire, domesticated, unbiting, and
with about as much life as a stuffed pet. Why? Because
relating to other people, loving them, is such a chore. How
much easier to sing a song at worship about the love of God
and then to trot off to my car alone rather than be bothered
to offer anyone a lift. If I ask around, then I may be
delayed; the conversation on the way home may not be
about what interests me. It's all an inconvenience. So I
keep my love clipped into the neat border of pansies
ringing the edges of my life. Whenever I let the Lord near
me, whenever I surrender my thinking about God to the
God of heart and flame, he tears this carefulness to shreds.
He takes the lid off my complacency and exposes me once
again, as he did Judith, to the seething vat of another me.

"The peace of God", I mutter wryly, is bought at the cost
of my own life, as once again I'm sent exploring another
facet of the inner turmoil. I am not alone. True God speaks
to true self, and the conversation is tongued in fire. This
God is not cosy and this experience is red in tooth and claw.
But it's all happened before. I love the Psalms, they blaze
with the flames of true self laid bare before true God. In
them there is no room for pseudo-innocence, pseudo-con-
cern and pseudo-devotion. It's the pitched battle of life and
death. Listen to some of the skirmishes:

> Thou hast hurled us back before the enemy,
> and our foes plunder us as they will.
> Thou hast given us up to be butchered like sheep . . .
>
> (Psalm 44:10–11)

or

The voice of the Lord makes flames of fire burst forth . . .
The Lord makes the wilderness of Kadesh writhe.

(Psalm 29:8)

or

> My iniquities have overtaken me,
> and my sight fails . . .
>
> (Psalm 40:12)

and

> Lord, make haste to answer,
> for my spirit faints.
> Do not hide thy face from me
> or I shall be like those who go down to the abyss.
>   (Psalm 143:7)

The Lord calls us to an abundance of life, and this means a
struggle in the depths of ourselves. The false, little self is
always in conflict with the true self seeking to be born.
There is no birth without change. All change involves not
only possibility but loss, and threat of loss sets up our
desire to possess. So part of a growing response to God is to
allow his Spirit to lead us into areas of conflict and tension
and extreme discomfort.

How do we react to this?

Our reaction often is not directly to the inner conflict
but to the change in our relationship with others that it
brings. Perhaps when we felt bathed in the light of God
others were attracted to us, and even sought our advice on
prayer or problems. Now we're not so free as we were.
We're somewhat preoccupied with the darkness that God's
light has shown up. Now people don't come to us so much.
At first we might not notice. We've been looking at the
Lord for long enough to be more concerned with him
rather than with our own popularity or lack of it. But
slowly, our sight of the Lord is clouded over by our preoccupation too and, with a final stumble into blindness, we
become trapped into wondering what other people are
thinking about us, or how we can influence them.

Need

Then, like one of the foolish girls in Jesus' parable, we
scuttle round with empty lamps, not content to sit alone in
the dark, but trying hard to foist our emptiness on to
others. Before, others needed us and we gave freely. Now
we need others to bolster up our self-esteem. So off we go,

giving words of knowledge when they're not asked for and dishing out advice to those who don't want it. We busy-body, trying to do good, and forget that do-ing good is an uprooted, withered plant unless it springs from the soil of be-ing good. How often have you ducked from a do-gooder, the sort of person who steamrollers you with his advice and knowledge and insensitivity? We may not be able to put it into words, but we sense that such a person is concerned, not so much with our good, but with his own.

All we ever have to give is ourselves. If that self is in conflict, then all we can give is conflict and restlessness. If we are empty, then all we can give is our emptiness.

This is real suffering for those who have wanted God enough to enter into battle and emptiness. As the little, false "I" asserts itself again, so it brings with it all the sense of isolation and alienation that we thought the felt presence of God had healed. We feel as if the glowing cords that bind everything together in God are fading and fraying.

Responsibility

Another way I so often react is to blame other people for not providing the satisfaction and help that I feel I need. I can ask for advice and then dismiss what help is given as insufficient or off the point. And I'm not alone in this. Not long ago, I heard a conversation between two young women after a church service. The first young woman announced, "We've been invited to a wedding next week and I haven't anything to wear. Tony has said I can buy something new."

"Where are you going to look?"

"I don't know. Tony said I could go to one of the new shops in town."

"Have you thought of . . .? You'd look lovely in their things."

"No, I haven't. You really think they might suit me?" the first young woman asked.

"Yes. But they're quite pricey. Don't look there unless you're prepared to dig into your pocket."

"Oh, that's OK. Tony said I could have a treat." They were talking again the following week.

"The wedding was beautiful."

"Did you enjoy your new dress?" her friend asked.

"Yes. But it cost more than I expected. I had to ring Tony from the shop to check if it was all right."

"And he agreed?"

"Yes he did. But it was all your fault." Her friend smiled, not a bit put out by the accusation.

It certainly wasn't all her fault. She'd responded to a request for advice and given the warning that the outfit might prove expensive. The woman who went to the wedding was in two minds about her dress. She wanted it enough to buy it but, perhaps, she felt it wrong to spend the amount she had. Unable to accept the responsibility for what was her own decision (and, even then, she'd sought and acquired permission from her husband) she decided to offload the tension on to her friend with the "It was all your fault."

As we pray and so journey into the territory of our true selves, we learn to let others be themselves. We also learn to accept responsibility for ourselves. When our false self, the frightened, little "I" troubles us, we lose this ability. We start to try to manipulate God again; we use others, and we become reluctant to take responsibility for our decisions and actions. The strands of our spiritual life unravel, and fall slackly through our fingers. We ask of others what we should only ask of God, and then blame them when they fail to deliver the goods. We blunder around in the dark, calling for help. We shout so loudly that we drown any replies. Desperately, we grab, and in grabbing, we suffer what every greedy person suffers, the law of diminishing returns. We want so much that nothing satisfies us, and we become increasingly cut off.

Once we are alone again we need to bolster up the little "I"'s sense of importance. So we relapse into possession – my property, my money, my ideas, my causes, my ministry and my way of doing things. We become willing to destroy anything else in a desperate attempt to defend what is mine. The spirit which starts by blaming a friend with "It's all your fault," is the same spirit which, in the past, racked and burned those of differing viewpoint. It is the spirit which ends up launching rockets or bombs in Northern Ireland or Palestine today.

A trouble shared may be a trouble halved but it may be ducking the issue. It is easy to moan to others and to relieve tension by a good heart to heart. At times this can be right but at times, also, it can obstruct the Spirit's work in us. The experience of great tension or discomfort may be his promptings to rework some imaginative exercises or readings from the Bible. Keeping our own counsel and doing this can sometimes lead us towards relationship and connection at deeper levels than we've experienced before. St. Paul tells us that the power of the Spirit in us is the same power that raised Jesus from the dead. This power seeks to raise us too, at the deepest levels of our responses and our desire for love.

Prayer and sexuality

Whenever we are setting off for a part of the country we've not been to before, along with the suitcases, maps, travel sickness tablets and quiz games, an indispensable book goes with us into the car. This book is a mine of information about the history, points of interest and facilities of most of the towns and villages in England. It doesn't mince its words, describing some places as "congested" or "ruined by development". I'm quite sorry for one little town which suffers with an introduction of "And now we come to . . . and there is no escape."

I feel a little like that now that I'm coming to write about the relationship between the love of God and our sexuality. It's a case of "And now we come to sexuality, and there is no escape!"

The Bible never looks for an escape. All our talk about God can only be in language about our world and our life as we experience it. One of the richest of life's experiences, for the writers of scripture, was the experience of their sexuality. Some of their words take the form of the finest poetry. Listen to the writer of the Song of Songs:

You have stolen my heart, my sister,
you have stolen it, my bride,
with one of your eyes, with one jewel of your necklace.
How beautiful are your breasts, my sister, my bride!
Your love is more fragrant than wine . . .
Your lips drop sweetness like the honeycomb, my bride,
Syrup and milk are under your tongue . . .
                                        (Song of Songs 4:9–11)

The entire Song is a love poem between bride and groom, and the book closes with a final invitation from the bride to her bridegroom:

Come into the open, my beloved,
and show yourself like a gazelle or a young wild goat
on the spice-bearing mountains.
                                        (Song of Songs 8:14)

Throughout the Old Testament, the people of God are called his Bride. Jesus frequently referred to himself as a bridegroom. He related the presence of the bridegroom to the experience of joy. Some Pharisees asked him why his disciples didn't fast as John's did, and he replied, "Can you expect the bridegroom's friends to go mourning while the bridegroom is with them? The time will come when the bridegroom will be taken away from them; that will be the time for them to fast." (Matthew 9:15) But Jesus wasn't married, so how could he describe himself as a bridegroom? He confuses the issue further when he rejects any claims of exclusivity for family life including the claims of his own immediate family. Once, when he was talking to a crowd, word came that his mother and brothers wanted to speak to him. He replied, "Who is my mother? Who are my brothers?" And, looking round at those who were sitting with him, said, "Here are my mother and my brothers. Whoever does the will of God is my brother, my sister, my mother." (Mark 3:34–35)

It is left to the writers of the rest of the New Testament to supply Jesus with a bride. The bride chosen is the people who respond to God through him. John the Baptist is the first to equate love of Jesus with bridal love. He says, "I am not the Messiah; I have been sent as his forerunner. It is the bridegroom to whom the bride belongs." (John 3:29) The theme is taken up in the vision of John related in Revelation, "I saw the holy city, new Jerusalem, coming down out of Heaven from God, and ready like a bride adorned for her husband." (Revelation 21:1–2) It is the Spirit and the bride, who, in the same vision, plead with Jesus to "Come".

So, the Bible delights in sexuality as one of God's greatest gifts and pleasures for us. We see in the life of Jesus that exclusive, possessive family relationships are to be discouraged, and we find that Jesus, the unmarried, is described as the bridegroom to his people, who are the bride. How does this affect us when we pray?

God is the bringer of reality. As soon as we enter into prayer, we discover that it is neither an escape from the world nor an escape from ourselves. Sooner or later, the Spirit will even stop us using it as an escape from God. We are sent out from prayer to see the world more intently, and, in the light of God, to see ourselves more intently. Some may enter rapidly into the sort of integration of the personality which the Lord calls "wholeness" or holiness. Others experience more difficulty. For some, the difficulties arise from or affect their sexuality.

God is life, and life is energy. As Jesus tells us, he comes to bring us an abundance of life. Sometimes this abundance can be hard to cope with. The life of God growing in us is met with the life of the self. St. Paul moaned about this, ". . . what I do is not what I want to do, but what I detest." (Romans 7:15) As we try to respond more fully to the life of the Spirit in us, then the energies of our false self tend to assert themselves quite strongly too.

Some of those most experienced in prayer have been those most aware of these energies in themselves. Teresa of Avila, a very practical lady and a great friend of God, was also extremely attractive when young. She had "it", that indefinable something that encouraged men to buzz round her like bees round a honeypot. She learned, for the love of God in her fellow human beings, to harness and draw back her powers of attraction.

Perhaps the attraction is partly the result of prayer. Those who pray grow in love, they start to fall in love with God and then with the whole of life. Love is always attractive because, when somebody loves us, we feel valuable. Those who journey towards God, journey towards love. As all love springs from the love of God, it's quite easy for people to get their sexual and their other love responses mixed up for a while. Our sexuality sneaks in under the guise of our happiness at being accepted by someone.

The growth towards God may heighten some people's sexual awareness for another reason. The Bible's analogy of the person's relationship with God being akin to that of bride and groom, may provide a key here. We love because love is the hallmark of God's craftsmanship in us. It's the "made in Heaven" and the "made for Heaven" with which we're all branded. For many of us, married or not, some of our most intense experiences of love have been sexual. It starts with the teenage crush and may or may not, later, take the form of marriage. But can you remember your early fantasies about someone of the opposite sex? That fluttering in the stomach when you saw him or her; the breathlessness; the longing to get to know her; the half dreamed of, half feared terror of a first kiss? For those who do marry, there's the experience of sexuality in intercourse, that indescribable loss of self in a completion which is the relationship experienced by the two of you. The loss of self can be so complete that the French have an apt name for intercourse. They term it "the little death". We speak of "drowning" in love and the pledge of lovers is the oft repeated "All that I have is yours and yours and yours."

For some, these facets of human love become a pale reflection of the love they experience from God and for God. It's no longer their sexuality which provides the greatest sense of fullness of relationship but their being held in God in a completion beyond words or pictures or imagination. The love of God is experienced as the face to face exchange of love. Sexuality asserts itself as a sort of echo or mirror image of that love. All this finds expression in the bride/bridegroom imagery of the Bible but it can be quite a problem to the person who prays. It can take time to bring peace to sexual energy in the growth of the love experienced in God.

Peace grows from tension. The tension may take the form of sexual flaunting such as flirtation. But for those in the sexual relationship of marriage it may, for a while, take the form of an unresolved battle of loyalty to God and loyalty to the marriage partner. This is not a flight from our sexuality to God as from something impure to the Pure. Our sexuality is so good that it, above all, is both the mirror of our love of God and, for some, the mirror from which they wish to turn to experience the source of love alone. The desire to channel all our sexual energy into our love for God poses fewer problems if we experience it before marriage. As Jesus said, ". . . there are others who have themselves renounced marriage for the sake of the kingdom of Heaven. Let those accept it who can." (Matthew 19:12).

For those who are already married and, through prayer, experience a shift in the central focus of their life, there may be a time of disruption and suffering for both marriage partners. But, from such a disruption, peace and integration and a new creativity will grow once the lover has "settled" into God. In fact, a full entry into the joys and potential of a marriage is dependent on neither of the partners being God for the other but is dependent on both partners accepting their relationship with joy as a pledge and mirror of the love of God. Ultimately, all love is of God and all love can lead to God. No love can rival God.

Father, let us not be afraid of who we are
Help us to trust you when we meet tension within
   ourselves
Forgive us when we blame others for our own failings
Help us to know that it is you who is speaking to us in our
   battles
Teach us to take time and to explore what you are saying.

9

GETTING DISTRACTED

When I read something like the last chapter or, worse still, when I live it, life can seem little more than heavy and complicated. What's the age-old answer to our heaviness in life? For a lot of us, it's escapism. The vocabulary of flight is etched into our language. We talk of "burying ourselves in a good book"; "escaping into another world" when we read a novel; or of "drowning our sorrows in drink". Some dream dreams on drugs and others get lost in a good film. The tension between what we'd hoped for in life and what we experience sets up intolerable anxieties and disappointments in us and we compensate ourselves for the pain we're feeling.

It starts early on. I knew a child once who, whenever things got tough, raided the biscuit tin or grabbed anything to hand which would literally sweeten the situation for her. So if too many guests were in the house, threatening her special place in the family, she wolfed at least two biscuits. On the day before she was due to start school the medicine cabinet lost its reserve tube of throat pastilles. The dog's birthday bar of chocolate paid off the dread of moving house and school. Before we smile and compliment ourselves on having outgrown such obvious compensations let's ask, how often do I take flight from reality in daydreams? The popularity of the most recent outcrop of films and TV dramas showing "rags to riches" stories of success and acquisition, indicates that we're all in the sweetening business. If my life is drab, poor and routine, I turn on the box and get lost in the wealth and intrigue of the lives of others.

There's a story dating from sixteenth-century Bohemia which talks about daydreams. There was once a poor peasant woman who was taking some eggs to market. On the way she started to daydream. If only I had a cock and a hen, she thought, I could have a lot more chickens. And then, if I had a lot more chickens, I could sell some and buy a cow. Eventually, with the produce from the cow, I could earn enough to buy a horse. At the prospect of buying a horse, she became so excited that she jumped up and down and broke all the eggs in her basket!

God is the bringer of reality. Whilst we're experiencing battle in our lives we may find ourselves trying to run away from the demands of reality. Our daydreams will take the form of whatever gives us most compensation. They may be religious. Without thinking, I may find myself imagining I'm one of the leaders in the church, or that God has chosen me for some special ministry. Perhaps I invent an entire alternative life for myself. I'm a missionary or a monk or an evangelist. Maybe I just conjure up a time of peace which has avoided conflict. A friend told me of just such a temptation she experienced not long ago. She was in evening service when she caught sight of a woman whom she disliked, sitting in a pew opposite. She felt that any worship she might try to offer the Lord was exploding into shards of resentment and irritation and anger. I'd be much better off at home, she thought, singing hymns there or listening to a cassette. Then she decided that would be ducking the issue. She told me, "You can't hide from your tensions with other people and hope they'll go away. You have to go through them to God." Then another thought struck her, "Perhaps, they are, in fact, part of God."

Very often I just long for that attractive state of having arrived without undergoing the trouble of getting there. Then it's easy to console myself with Christian biographies, reading about what God has done in the lives of others as a substitute for the hard, creative work of allowing God to continue his uncomfortable work in my life now.

Prayer time can become fun again as I hook all my thoughts and imaginings to me and follow them along the route which takes me straight back to the false, comfort-loving, power-hungry "I". It doesn't feel as if I'm doing that. It feels as if I'm building castles in the air and inhabiting them. It feels like this, because this is what it is! God is not "pie in the sky when you die". God is here and now in whatever circumstances I find myself. It is just such here and now-ness which is too uncomfortable for me to live in.

God wants to make me more fully human. Often when I'm trying to escape him, I try to become more religious. I may run to every church meeting and conference, read religious books, fly from listening to people into swapping God talk with them and desperately seek the company of those whom I believe to be "like minded". I use all this clutter to build a dry stone wall to keep God out. Anything rather than continue the now boring, tedious discipline of bringing the powers of my imagination and spirit under the discipline of God's Spirit.

My retreat from God may not take the form of daydreaming myself into religious soft options. It may just be a retreat into the old times where the grass now looks so much greener. Whatever I dreamt about then, I dream about now; holidays, world tours, a better house, those velvet curtains I've set my heart on, or the job three rungs up the ladder that I've been after for years.

I can travel back, sighing, "Ah, wasn't it all so much easier/lovelier/more hopeful then?" And I can travel forward into the "wouldn't it be lovely" country, clambering over the foothills of the "if only . . ." range on the way. And what effect does this have on the way I look at the pile of washing-up in the sink, or the pile of papers on my desk, the baby's teething problems or my husband's dirty socks? It makes it doubly difficult for me to accept God in my circumstances here and now. Sometimes we invest all our disappointment in one enormous daydream of the "if only I were married/in a convent/living somewhere else, it would all be different" kind. I find I can invent innumerable ways to shut out the gentle, persistent knocking of God here and now, in my life as it is, on a tired afternoon in February with sleet dissecting the tea time gloom.

Earlier on I mentioned learning something about discerning my moods. Over some years, and with the help of jottings from my prayer diary, I've found analysing my escapist tendencies – When do they bother me? What brings them on? What form do they take? – has helped me to be more responsive to the Holy Spirit when he's trying to prompt me back on track. It even took me some time to realise how much I daydreamed before I could start to sift the contents of what I dreamed about. Sifting has helped me to become more aware of unhelpful escapism but also of positive moods. Gradually, I'm beginning to discover a little more of the path of salvation which winds somewhat narrowly among the tantalising cul de sacs of areas in my inner life. These cul de sacs usually stretch out before me, at first sight like three-lane motorways, and I'm still likely to be speeding at seventy in the outside lane before I catch a glimpse of the dead end ahead!

When St. Paul was writing to the church at Philippi he talked about being thoroughly initiated into the human lot. He gives us an insight into the fruits of learning to recognise what is constructive and what is destructive in ourselves when he explains, ". . . I have learned to find resources in myself whatever my circumstances. I know what it is to be brought low, and I know what it is to have plenty. I have been thoroughly initiated into the human lot with all its ups and downs". (Philippians 4.12) As the Holy Spirit brings tensions and uncertainties to light, as he probes our desires and daydreams, perhaps he also enlarges our sympathies. We discover the dark in ourselves and God's Spirit tells us the discovery is all right. We learn to have compassion on ourselves. It is to those who are troubled and uncertain, but still longing for God, to whom Jesus says he brings good news. It is only the complacent and satisfied to whom he gives the reminder that life in God demands total change. Jesus accepts us, and because he accepts us we can begin to accept ourselves. Only then can we begin to accept our brothers and sisters without fear. It is only as the Spirit shows me that I am a coward and violent, lazy and a daydreamer, and that God loves me, that I love the sad and violent, lazy world both inside and outside myself.

Jesus was all light but he was all light because his light had illuminated the darkness not because his light had failed to turn in that direction at all. Equally, it was by forgiving his executioners that he drew the poison of hatred from their action and turned it into an offering of his love. The Jesus who reconciled and integrated his personality is the Jesus who tells us to love others as we love ourselves. The Jesus who was tempted begs us to forgive. It is only as we forgive others that God can forgive us. We will only be able to forgive others when we can rejoice in being forgiven. To do this we have to learn to forgive ourselves. Forgiveness is the philosopher's stone which takes the dross or base metal in our personality and, by the heat of love, transfigures it into the gold of the developing likeness of God in us.

As we learn to recognise the good and bad in ourselves, and to forgive ourselves, so we cease to judge others. None is good but God alone and, at last, even we can see that our heavenly Father makes his sun rise on good and bad alike, and sends rain on the honest and dishonest. And that the heavenly Father's goodness knows no bounds.

Holy Spirit, spread out the wings of your compassion in me

Help me to see that what I dislike in the world lives in me

Help me to love my darkness into your light, and so, to take your light into the world.

10

JOURNEYING INTO THE NIGHT

So far, the conflict we may have experienced is a conflict within ourselves. That self is alive and kicking, and fighting the Spirit of God for a life of its own spirit. We may be "such stuff as dreams are made on" but we have refused to go to sleep. However, dreams and sleep and death are closely related. It is through dreams that God sometimes communicates with us; it is in sleep that our conscious self gives up its fight to assert itself. In sleep the "I", that thinks and eats and works and plays, surrenders itself. St. Paul likened this surrender to death when he described the Christian dead as those who are "asleep in the Lord".

So it's not surprising that, when the Spirit of God has led us through the journey of our escapist dreams, he leads us into a deeper sleep which, for some of us, feels like non-existence. There's a song which was popular a few years ago with the words "killing me softly". That might be a good description of this stage of the journey.

We've faced conflict and we've taken side-tracks but we've still, even if it's only been from time to time of late, sensed something of the presence of God. He's still there holding us, if only we can stop wriggling long enough to feel his arms. We can still love him and stretch out to others as we recognise their weakness in ourselves. But there comes a time when all this goes into shutdown. Then we try to pray and there's nothing there. We look round the room and the walls are the walls whilst the ceiling looms over us. It's all foursquare and solid and cold. Where are the angels and archangels? Wherever they are, they are not caring for me! Where is my love, my joy, my hope? They've faded away. I sit by the grey ashes of a once glowing fire, growing cold. I start to shiver. And, most of all, where is God? I start to pray and I can't find him. He isn't there, and I'm alone. I huddle in fear. Then indignation – it's not fair. I've done nothing to deserve this. I could understand if I'd deliberately sinned. Then I know I shut you out, God. But it's not like that. I've asked the Holy Spirit to sift my heart and I can't discover any poison which is lurking there, seeping through my life and killing my loves.

I'm trying to pray as usual; I'm reading my Bible; I'm singing hymns. True, I'm having difficulty thinking about God at all. But then I've had difficulty thinking about God since I started this kind of prayer. Long ago, when I first came into your presence in silence, you became much too big to be packaged by my intellect. It's getting worse; now I'm having difficulty using my imagination. I can't burrow to the centre of Jesus' stories any longer and his words shrink from me, dusty letters on a stained page. I repeat, this is not fun. I've not given up on you, God, but it's beginning to feel terribly as if you've deserted me. I'm alone. I'm afraid, more afraid than I've ever been. I want to connect but people seem distant. Life is becoming very flat, and I'm strung out on that flatness, getting thinner and less interested. Yes, that's it: I'm bored. I'm afraid and cut off and bored. This is like dying: it's all gloomy; no light, no gaiety, no comfort any more. Is this what you want of me, God?

I once had a dream which pictured some of this for me. In my dream, I walked along a garden path, a greying, gentle path with soft tufts of moss cushioning the corners of the stones. Arches of roses sprang together over my head and the air grew heavy with their June freshness. At the end of the tunnel of roses stood a final arch. It was built massively of blocks of stone and strange lettering was etched on the lintel. I could not understand the writing but the word glowed to me like an invitation. As I slipped through the arch, I felt lighter. I began to skip. I came to a large meadow of sap-oozing grass scattered with wild flowers. The grass hadn't been mown but there was about it that

tangy smell of recent cutting. I began to run and dance
through the meadow.

Then I was back on the tunnel path again. I realised I
hadn't gone through the field and out the other side.
Somehow, I knew there wasn't another side; the meadow
just got better, the grass sweeter and my joy more intense.

But that was memory. The path now was different. This
time the roses didn't greet each other overhead. They
hung limp on the briars, full-blown and exuding that
sickly, overripeness of ageing summer. The moss under my
feet pressed into my soles, dry and brittle, and the thorns,
which I hadn't noticed before on the rose stems, snatched
at me, scratching arms and legs. I tried to run and
couldn't, feeling heavy and dull. It wasn't that I'd grown
old, just that the joy had ebbed from me, leaking slowly
away like water down an ill-fitting plug hole. I ploughed on
along my now joyless path to the massive arch at the end.
As I approached and looked up for the lettering, the marks
on the lintel faded into a chilling absence of welcome. It
was if a crowd of beckoning friends suddenly grew silent,
looked through me and then turned their backs. Nothing.

I dragged myself nearer. Now I was almost at the arch.
This time, despite being close, I couldn't see through to the
other side. Then the supports, on either side of the opening, sprouted wood. The wood creaked rapidly across the
gap and, as I reached to touch them, the wooden barriers
closed against each other. In a final sealing, the line of the
join wobbled, then faded away entirely.

I stood in front of a perfectly smooth barrier of exclusion.
Perhaps if I pushed? I put out my hand to feel it. It was real
all right. I pushed. It didn't give. Then I started to explore
the wood. The surface felt glossily uniform to my finger-
tips, neither hot nor cold. Merely indifferent. It wasn't for
me or against me. It was just massively *there*. Slowly, my
fingertips explored the entire surface, searching for a
hole, a knot, an indentation, anything on which I could get
leverage. Nothing. The world diminished to the size of
the barrier and me . . .

For now, let's leave me there, standing alone and

excluded, with a sense of hopelessness I hadn't experienced before.

How can it be that the God of love, who is always communicating himself, can lead us into a place of desolation? A place where we are deaf and dumb, where no birds sing, no flowers grow and no hands stretch out to help us? A place where silence no longer supports us but locks against us like a wall? It swallows our cries and our whispers alike, so that we open our mouths and our words are as if they'd never been. Our lives feel cold, our heart and mind frostbitten almost to the core.

Is this love? Yes, this is love. This is the love which cannot be survived. This is the love that leads to death. And deep down, we've suspected this before. There comes a point when love consumes, when the flames of love can't be survived.

Christ in us

This is the love which killed Jesus. ". . . not as I will but as thou wilt", he cried to his Father. (Matthew 26:39) It is the love which killed St. Paul: "All I care for is to know Christ, to experience the power of his resurrection, and to share his sufferings, in growing conformity with his death, if only I may finally arrive at the resurrection from the dead." (Philippians 3:10) and in Galatians, "I am crucified with Christ". (Galatians 2:20) This gives us a clue. Scripture assures us that we have the mind of Christ. Alarming and wonderful as it may seem, God wants us to be like Christ.

So far, the Holy Spirit has led us in our journey of prayer through the joy of the birth and the growth of Christ in us. This may have found its fullest expression in those facets of the jewel of communion with God that we experienced at times. This is a little like God's affirmation of Jesus in his baptism. We sensed, however unworthy we felt, that God was pleased with us. And then there has been ministry. But Jesus was tempted; and we have been tempted. We have become aware of the strength and depths of our spirits when the Holy Spirit has taught us through conflict and tension.

Now, we start to experience the absence of God although we desire his presence as much as ever. This is a faint shadowing of the death of Christ. Jesus' death was a demonstration of his love. Death was not easy for Jesus; he dreaded it. On the cross he experienced that extreme of alienation we call despair, "My God, my God, why hast thou forsaken me?" (Mark 15:34) Our going down to death is not the same as Jesus'. We are not asked to be the channel by which God draws the sin of the world into his love where all its darkness may be made light. Nevertheless, we are asked to surrender ourselves in a form of trust that is new to us. We may find we don't experience something as powerful as despair but something much more like that cold, wet, unappetising fish of the ebbing of hope.

Someone was telling me of a couple of stays in hospital which she had last year. Through these the Lord accomplished just the same sense of alienation and helplessness. The first thing to go, she said, was the structure for prayer. She was in a great deal of pain and just didn't have the strength or energy to read systematically or to prepare herself as she had before. Prayer became a series of short exclamations, a little like those St. Francis was sometimes heard to use – "My God and my All". The Psalms also came back to her in part. Long years of Bible reading gave her a reservoir on which to draw when it was no longer possible to read.

The illness was serious and she was absolutely helpless and dependent on others for the smallest service, from a bedpan to a drink of water. She learnt to know the nurses by their touch, she said. In fact, all the senses became extremely important. Flat on her back, her world was restricted to the sight of a single flower in a vase by her bed, or someone's hand holding her own.

At first she felt angry at the lack of control over her life and circumstances. Acceptance didn't come easily. But when she did accept, what Jesus had said in the gospels became true for her. As someone gave her a cup of water, she felt the love of God for her; the quiet companionship of a visitor was part of God's presence.

She said she felt the physical pain terribly, and hated that – the pain and the helplessness. She couldn't "overcome" the pain, only offer that to God, align her "little pain" (her words) to Christ's suffering on the cross.

She was too weak and exhausted for words. That, too, spoke to her. She was reminded that what Jesus experienced on the cross was also beyond words. There was a strong sense of her own death, not only in the obvious sense, but in a host of little ways. She was kept in the dark; people did things to her without telling her why. She was washed or not washed at their beck and call. Her world diminished to a crumpled bed sheet under her and the gnawing anxiety in her. How long would it be like this? When could she go home? Would she ever be all right again? And everyone else carried on with their normal, competent, controlling lives.

The absence of God

What do we feel like doing when God becomes absent to us?

Perhaps we sense panic rising, and scurry off to chat to others about it. We feel there must be ways we can encourage (force?) the Lord to return to us, if only someone will give us a clue. But a sickness to the death, we discover, is beyond the cure of even the most sympathetic friend. If your friend is wise, he'll leave you to God's devices in this, anyway. We may feel like giving up, returning to our life as it was and salvaging what we can of contentment or happiness.

This is how I felt. After about a month of the absence of God, I thought, "enough is enough", got up off my knees, dusted myself down and decided to pick up the threads of the rest of my activity, having dropped prayer from the various skeins which wove my life.

But it wasn't that easy. God had become like a black hole for me. I first heard about black holes on the TV. They are thought to be areas of immense density and of a gravity so fierce that even light cannot escape its pull. The scientist who was talking explained that this pull was so strong that it attracted everything within thousands of miles, drawing it into a centre of dense nothingness. That rang bells with my experience of the absence of God. I stopped praying and tried to put my energy into the rest of my life. I'd always enjoyed academic work so I picked up books again. I loved material and line and set out to design clothes for our daughters. I'd sometimes designed Christmas cards and determined to do so again this season.

That was the plan. However, during my years of prayer, I'd given my past to God – loss which had hurt, now hurt in his love; ambitions were dampened by his Spirit, and my desire for him had blunted my appetite for study, which I had previously gobbled, fact after fact, like a box of chocolates. The academic work which had excited me before, for its own sake, now tasted dry as dust; the dressmaking fell apart at the seams, and I didn't get round to starting the cards. Like a black hole, God had attracted all my past, and those things which I'd enjoyed before. These, too, were swallowed by his absence. Wryly, I reflected, they would be, wouldn't they? God is the "I will be" – nothing is ever static and one is never allowed to go back. The call of the Holy Spirit is, "Walk on". So, much that I knew about myself was eaten by the black hole of emptiness too. I was no longer the person who sewed, studied, made cards. Who I was would only materialise as I walked on. And the problem of walking on was the age-old problem of confidence. The obvious trouble with the future is that it hasn't happened yet. So it is potentially unsafe. I began to experience little rats' claws of anxiety scurrying up and down my spirit.

The last, remaining comforts of familiarity were removed when we upped stakes and travelled from the West to the East of the country when my husband started a new job. Moving house was a wrenching pain for me because I had fallen in love with where we lived when we were newly married. I grieved for the place as I would for a person. The No God of my inner life was echoed by the breaking of pattern in my everyday outer life. I flapped around like a fish out of water, my mouth opened and closed in a desperate search for life in this alien territory.

This all felt too much. I decided to do something about it. The usual complaint of people who start the prayer of silence is that, because of the way God starts to use them, they run into difficulties about finding time for prayer. When I felt the call of God, however busy I was with young children, studying and a part-time job as well as people popping in, I found time to be silent before the Lord. Now, however, time was the last thing I wanted. All I was concerned to do was to put the emptiness behind me, to build bridges across the yawning chasms of God's absence, even though I knew they were bridges of hay and straw. For me, when love had departed, all there was was a filling up of time. Anything to lessen the pain, anything to stifle the memories! I joined groups, I took on more work, I became busier and busier in an attempt to weave a covering, no matter how threadbare, over the gap and the pain of my life. I also needed to compensate for a loss of value. For years, my value had been given by God. Now, no God, no value, or at best, a drastic reduction in confidence.

Stability

After a couple of years of this, a very wise Christian intervened. "Yes, it is like being a fish on a hook lying gasping on the bank," he agreed. But added, "Squeal as much as you like. Wriggle round but don't try to get off the hook."

So I began the slow, painful drawing of this experience into a God who, for all I knew, didn't receive it. The absence stood solid. Odd things helped, like one line of poetry which I discovered. The short poem described how God had taken all the poet's comfort but, at the end, the writer asserts:

If all is lost, thanks be to God,
For He is He, and I, I am only I.

This somehow put things into focus. It is God, not I, who is the centre of the universe. My job is to follow him as best I can, to allow him to be with me and in me in the way he wants, not the ways I prefer. "I am only I."

I began reading scripture again – systematically meditating on the words, sucking them slowly like a fruit drop, so that the taste could trickle down into my life. I found I could no longer use my imagination in the service of prayer. My imagination had other work. First it grieved for the loss of a place which I had loved so much. It took two or three years for it even to make the slow crawl from the West to the East of England. When it did arrive, it busied itself in the areas of dance and teaching and writing. If I tried to exercise it in prayer, it went rigid on me. So I let it go. I had no idea what God might be doing. Did he? I wondered sometimes.

In the periods of agonising silence, where time now limped and stumbled, where once it had pleated into the present moment, I sent darts of love to the Lord. I again repeated the phrases I'd used so long before, "My Lord and my God" or "My God and my All". Unsure of any recipient, I offered myself.

Sometimes the Lord gave glimpses, often in response to offering. Love invokes love and I got just enough sense of God to keep me sweet. It would be more accurate to say, to keep me from biting everybody's head off! God saw that I needed some generosity to keep going at all.

I continued to pray regularly, using written prayers, or lying flat on my front before the Lord. Study and prayer were again in some sort of place. I hadn't given up going to church, and to these I added a few simple ways of going out from myself to others. The mechanisms of spontaneous loving had ground to a halt, and I was determined not to inflict my emptiness on others, or to use them as a sort of convenience to distract me from myself. So I confined what I did to practical things like delivering the parish

magazines or to writing hand-outs for church functions.
I led at prayer meetings if asked but found it quite a
torture.

Gradually, throughout the next few months, the foundations of a life given to God were hewn out once more.
There were one or two newish pillars in the building
works. I was learning not to look for escape but to stay
with the emptiness. I was also learning what was very
difficult for me, not to look for so much stimulus outside
myself. I sat still to face some of the boredom and isolation
and feelings of waste or disappointment.

There again, sometimes I didn't. Anxiety was running
quite high and when it all got too much I scurried off into
busyness again. It was that sort of activity which masks
emptiness, not the activity which flows from prayer. And I
still do it sometimes.

All that remained was for the Lord to return to his
temple. There was nothing more I could do. That was his
decision. I had tried to go back and found that I couldn't.
Going forward was the work of the Holy Spirit and I didn't
know what was happening there. Standing still was the
best I could muster. And very often that collapsed into
scurrying.

Less is more

Looking back on her period in hospital my friend asked
herself what came out of it. She said that from the death of
her own peace of mind grew a much greater sense of the
connections between everyone. People literally ministered to her by their touch and by their presence. She also
learnt that almost everything that she had thought was
certain about herself was, in fact, terrifyingly fragile.
Where was her control? Gone. Her ability? Gone. Her
choices in life? Gone. So, what was left to trust in? Only
God. She hoped that, when health returned, she wouldn't
lose her vulnerability.

Looking back on my years of aridity, I can now ask the
question which I found almost too painful to ask at the

time – what is God doing when he seems to be absent from us for no good reason?

I suppose the short answer to that is that he is being formed in us in far greater depth. This needs room. Somebody has to move over, somebody has to die a little. Every death is a preparation for new birth. Birth to a new outlook on life is doubly painful. It involves the death of the old. Then comes the pain of the period of limbo, that awful, anxious not knowing that I have tried to put into words, when you feel as if you are suspended between the old loves which you knew and the yet unborn new loves, if there are to be any on offer. All that you are sure of is the depth of the chasm opening up beneath you. Finally, there is the pain of new birth.

Let's consider a moment something of the death of Jesus. His dying was itself part of his glorification by God. The resurrection was the outward sign that the Father had accepted the Son's life offered up to him.

The sense of the absence of God, which we feel as the death of his love in us, is itself part of our glorification. We are being moved from glory to glory, just as St. Paul tells us will happen. All our pain is the pain of being brought to a new birth, a resurrection. What is happening is that there is a further shift at the centre of our lives. When I first loved God, he gave the overwhelming joy of his presence, those glittering, diamond facets. The "I" that loved him was the old, emotional "I" with all its moods and fluctuations. Above all that "I" was devoted to its own comfort, especially its spiritual comfort. Now, all the ideals of that love had tarnished and lost their glow. God usually takes away our ideals because it is in our ideals that our old, little, false life is firmly entrenched. It doesn't matter whether the ideals are religious or not, just as it didn't matter whether our escapism was religious or not. So my full-bodied ideals of prayer and love shrivelled and dried out to hang like tattered shreds of flesh on the skeleton of a bony and uncomfortable life.

In all this aridity, God's creativity is undertaking a tunnelling work. As our emotions wither and desert us, he is burrowing away at the level of our wills. Will we love God, or will we love our experience of God? Will we follow God for his truth, or for our comfort? Will I really mean my offering of myself, that "anything, Lord", when that offering crucifies me? Will I? Will I? Will I?

We don't know the answer and, as we travel further into the dark, our helplessness increases. By helplessness, I don't mean inability to do things. We may still be one of the best plumbers or professors around. We may be a preacher in great demand or the person who can be relied upon to come up with ideas just when they're needed. The helplessness I'm talking about is that inability to find our satisfaction outside God. We can no longer rely on our achievements or qualifications or our past record to give us satisfaction. Increasingly we realise that if we don't have God, we have nothing. I mean nothing. This increasing helplessness is good. Now we are beginning to experience that it is in God that we exist and not in ourselves.

Our teenage daughter is full of her growing need for independence. When I ask her if she's packed her school bag for tomorrow, the fussiness of my question is dismissed with a curt, "Course I have!" It's the same with school uniform, preparation of food for Domestic Science lessons, learning of lines for the church pantomime. "Course I have!" is her cry of "Leave me alone, I can manage." She usually makes it clear too that now she knows far more than I do about anything that matters. In short, I am no longer necessary for her deepest satisfactions. But, earlier this year, she was tipped off balance. One of the final pantomime rehearsals was scheduled for 6.45 to 8.45 one January night. David, my husband, arranged to collect her from the church hall at 8.45. The organisers had forgotten that another group had booked the hall from 8.15 so, in confusion, the pantomime people began to trickle away at this time, half an hour earlier than planned. Our daughter was left bewildered and panicky on the hall steps until a very kind couple offered to bring her home. At first, she refused as she'd been taught to do, but then realised this couple had been at every rehearsal and were members of the church. She then accepted and, somewhat chastened, was delivered home at 8.30. There wasn't quite so much of the "Course I have" for a couple of weeks after that.

Most of us run calling on God when things go wrong but it takes a good dose of experience of our helplessness, even when we're functioning perfectly competently, to make us understand that, if God blinked, the universe would go out. As our longing increases, so we start to understand that we draw every breath in him. He is our food and our work; our rest and our play. As we long for him in his absence, so we realise our true self cannot exist without him.

"God whispers in our pleasures. He shouts in our pain." (C. S. Lewis) When we flex the muscles of our will to love him rather than ourselves, we start to tread a little more lightly on our ups and downs. Some days I'm happy; some days I'm sad; some tired and some, brimful of life. Sometimes things go well, sometimes badly; sometimes I get the bouquets, sometimes the brick bats. Everything changes; nothing remains the same. Underneath all this, at a level below my emotional responses, a new song is forming. It goes like this, "I will bless the Lord continually: his praise shall be always on my lips." (Psalm 34:1) Why? Because he is he, and I, I am only I. The centre is starting to shift. God is important in himself rather than in respect to my life. Praise is beginning to lose itself in worship. A truer me is poised to be born.

For some Christians, the centre shifts so far that not only are good and bad days received with the same praise to God but suffering becomes attractive. This isn't to say that suffering is good in itself, nor is it a form of masochism. What is unpleasant isn't chosen for its own sake; there's no stiff, medicinal upper lip which says, "If it's nasty, it must be good for me." Suffering becomes attractive as the flowering of such a love for God and for the world that the desire to join any experience to the love that Jesus showed on the cross remains as the single, most powerful desire in a life. So, Teresa Martin, a young Christian of twenty-two, asked a friend, "Would you like to know which are my Sundays and feast days? They are the days on which God sends me the greatest trials." A few days earlier, this same young woman had held another conversation with a friend.

"How do you manage," the friend asked, "always to remain happy and peaceful and even?"

"I wasn't always like that, " Teresa replied, "but ever since I gave up all self-seeking, I have led the happiest of lives."

I believe Teresa and I'd like to be like her. Scripture makes it so clear. It's a case of me or Christ. It's the simple law of "... where your treasure is, there will your heart be also." (Luke 12:34) It's so simple but it costs everything, and, in the day to day choices, I still so often opt for myself with all the unhappiness, tension, divided heart that that involves. So long as I bank my treasure in two separate accounts, so long will my heart remain divided. Such division is the legacy of anxiety. Love in its fullness casts out fear. When I can trust the fullness of God's love fully, then my heart will cease to be divided.

As we journey through the dark with a growing awareness of our helplessness, we learn to trust ourselves less. Those who live in the heart of God have learnt not to trust themselves an inch. Perhaps one of the reasons why St. Peter denied his Lord was because he trusted himself to be faithful. It's very releasing not to expect anything, including trust, of oneself.

Trust in God takes us on a journey into humility and poverty. Spiritual poverty is the opposite of possessiveness. We learn to sit lightly on our moods, and we possess ourselves less. When we possess ourselves less, we need to possess others less. Jealousy, ambition, the need to be needed, the desire to notch up bench marks, begin to fall away. They fall away because we have experienced two things.

1) We have experienced that everything passes. All these fluctuations are a kind of high-pitched buzzing, a surface noise humming tunes of success or failure. The tune comes and goes and sometimes gets loud enough to become interference. But, at depth, the continued speech within us is the Word of God struggling to be born in the increasing silence of our hearts.

2) We are not sure any longer who we are. That may sound strange or frightening but it is neither. I still know every day that I am a businessman or that I am redundant; I may be a mother or a nurse, single or married, aged twenty and white or sixty-five and black. But this is not what I am talking about. I am using "I" in terms of fixed identity. And a lot of that has been blown from me by the breath of God. Ideals, dreams, past, achievements, reputation and interests (for some, close relationships and long term hopes may be included too) have tumbled into the black hole of the absence of God.

So what is left to give us satisfaction? Precious little apart from the love of God. Perhaps now, we start to understand a little of what St. Paul felt when he exclaimed, "dying, we still live on; disciplined by suffering, we are not done to death; in our sorrows we have always cause for joy; poor ourselves, we bring wealth to many; penniless, we own the world." (2 Corinthians 6:10)

Humility

We also start to grow in humility. What is humility? Humility is to live in the truth; this includes living in the truth about myself. As I approach God in the dark, I learn more of the truth about myself. That truth is that I only exist in God. To know that is to experience humility. If I only exist in God, how can I demand that I should always feel happiness or the felt presence of God? He who pays the piper, calls the tune. It is up to God to decide what moods and experiences are best for me.

I also start to understand that I own nothing. I may be

naturally gifted, but "naturally" doesn't make a lot of
sense any longer. Consequently, I can no longer overlook
others because they don't, in my judgment, seem to be as
interesting, gifted, steady or quick as I am. My old values
have turned topsy turvy. There is nothing which I own by
right: everything is given, including any faith which I
may stir up in myself.

It was because he understood the givenness of everything, that St. Francis called poverty "My Lady". He
wanted to live in a world of physical as well as spiritual
poverty. Most of us are not called to such extreme forms of
simplicity or, if called, couldn't respond. However, as we
start to rely more on God, then inch by inch, chip by chip,
we let things go. My children no longer exist to be owned
by me: they are God's children first. Whatever people
think of me is OK. It changes rapidly in any case, blown
about by the winds of their desires as well as my actions.
Most of us will find some areas of our lives clinging to us
with all the tenacity of gold leaf. I have particular trouble
with energy. I have a lot of it and like to direct it. It's
difficult when an activity stops unexpectedly or when
something that's taken a lot of my interest comes to an
end. I would like to learn to use the sudden, unchosen,
lettings go in my life as promptings to learn a little more
poverty.

To be spiritually poor is to be free. If I own nothing, then
no one can take it from me. If I don't care what mood I'm in,
then I'm safe in the praises of my Lord; if ministry is
incidental to worship, then it doesn't matter who does it. I
don't have to be involved, do I?

From humility springs poverty; from poverty springs
freedom; and from freedom springs joy. That is why the
music of humility is the sound of laughter. Such laughter
is an echo of the laughter of Heaven, the merry company of
the saints. No wonder Jesus said, "You shall know the
truth, and the truth will set you free." (John 8:32) Knowledge of the truth is like all knowledge of God. It is not to
"know that" but it is to "be changed by". To know the truth
is to live in humility and, for some, to long for and to live in

obscurity. God has often buried his treasure deepest in hidden lives.

Faith, hope and love

St. Paul tells us that three things only last for ever: faith, hope and love. It is these three that we start to taste in what we think of as the absence of God. By continuing to pray we exercise our hope. Hope is not a kind of blind optimism, "if wishing would but make it so!" Our hope lies in God, whose promises of nearness, love and power never let us down. The centre of our hope shifts from our own personality. If you are naturally pessimistic, then you probably didn't have much hope to go on in the first place! It was only when I found darkness that I discovered that a lot of what I'd thought was hope in my character, perhaps owed more to good health and vitality. The darkness challenged me to look for the light of hope in God rather in circumstances or a good digestion. Hope is very necessary if we are to learn to pray for the extension of God's kingdom in the world. Hope will open our eyes to the circumstances of the world (hope is not naïve, it is not afraid to look at what is there, however unattractive, frightening or sad), but it will keep the vantage point of our looking firmly anchored in God. In short, we will look at the world as never before, but we will look with something of God's perseverance and urgency and love. Hope will give us reason for action, will prompt our actions and will help us to keep going once we've started some action.

Love, as we've seen, is not just a quiet, slumbering, domestic pussy cat. Love can be a devouring tiger that pounces and kills. Love is a consuming fire and a raging wind as well as a still, small voice. Love upsets the apple cart. Love is not always comfortable. It can irritate like a hair shirt, scouring skin and probing flesh. God is love. As love gets a grip on us, taking us up on our offering, we start to learn something else about love. We begin to experience its demand for constancy.

It's not natural for our love to be rock solid. We only have to look at the divorce statistics to see that! And it starts long before that. When we're young, we change friends every half hour. You can hear it in the school playground any day. "I'm going to sit by Lisa on the coach."

"But you said you'd sit by me."

"That was this morning."

"You're not my best friend now."

Ask yourself, how long do you keep your friends?

Even the apostles found stability difficult. Peter and Paul had more than one spat, and Paul and Barnabas fell out because Paul felt Mark to be unreliable.

It is because we have felt something of God's stickability and generosity, that we have come to him in prayer in the first place. Now he wants to burn his image of generous love a little deeper into us.

He has loved us before we loved him, and his love has been given freely, without price. "Come and buy," he has called. "Come without money." We have gazed a little at the love of God, and now it is time for us to find out if any of that love is reflected in us.

God loved me when I wasn't aware of him, when I couldn't have cared less. Do I love him now when it feels as if he's not there?

God keeps loving day in and day out. Can I start to do that?

God loves me into forgiveness. Do I forgive God for not being present to me? Am I angry, thinking I can catch him, hold him and dictate my terms to him?

God is where I live and move and exist. He is closer to me than I am to myself. Is this silence a way of showing me that? Is he closer to me than all my feelings? Is that what this numbness is telling me?

Can I learn to take my first, uncertain, baby footsteps in real love, in the blind love we call faith? Or am I still tied to my feelings and my thoughts, using them as a borrowed light to guide myself?

At this point of perseverance love merges into faith. If you look at the well-known story that Jesus told about the sower and the seed, you'll find, at the end, a little comment about perseverance. Jesus, as recorded in Luke 8:15, explains that the good soil represents those who bring good and honest hearts to the hearing of the word, hold it fast, and, "by their perseverance, yield a harvest." The yielding of the harvest depends on the perseverance. The seed of the love of God that has rested in my emotions has to become bedded deeper in the dark soil of my will, far from the light. There, in coolness and in silence, the seed can germinate. Without germination, there can be no lasting, robust growth, leading to blossom and rich fruit.

It is in coldness and in silence that I learn the stick-ability from which God can bring harvest. It is only as I persevere that I can become of more use to God and to others. How long do I stand as a bridge of intercession in prayer? One or two days? Where's my perseverance? There's a lot of the "grit your teeth and get on with it" about love – a definite understanding that, after that initial spark of inspiration (call it attraction, falling in love, or what you like), we're called to answer with 99% perspiration. You can't be a disciple, one who follows the call to "Come" without discipline. Jesus persevered to the end. The final cry of perseverance was also a cry of triumph. It was the "It is completed" of the cross. The Lord has poured much sweetness, like honey, over my experience of him. But too much honey sickens; it also rots the teeth. Can I now eat the body building food of plain bread? Do I love God, or do I love my own feeling?

And so, love has fused with faith. In the spiritual life, we tend to reap what we sow. We find that the reward of faith is not sight. It is more faith. "I trust and I give," is not answered with, "Here I am so that you no longer have to trust and give." It is answered by a "Thank you" which resounds through our life and leads us to trust and give more. Faith is not fatalism. It is the fuel that powers more concern. Faith prompts us to act in co-operation with God; it enables us to launch out where we have been afraid.

Faith is what keeps us going forward. This is why all the greatest actions of God's people have been carried out through faith. Our faith is a tiny reflection of the going forward in faith of the great "I will be who I will be." Perhaps, once we start to enter into the blindness of deeper faith, we never quite regain our sight?

> Lord, help me to trust you
> when I no longer see you.
> May I know that it is
> Love that is blinding me
> and leading me to greater faith.

11

ON TRACK

One day, a rather stupid puppy dog asked its mother, "Mum, what is this air I breathe that I've heard so much about?"

She said to him, "You silly, little puppy dog. It's all around you and inside you. If you want to find out what it's like, just stop lapping your milk and sink your head in a pail of the stuff. You'll soon find out."

On the same day, a pretty but dim small fish swam up to its mother and said to her, "Mummy, I've listened when fish talk about water – but I don't know what it is. What is water?"

"You silly little sprat," she replied. "Water is all about you. It's inside you." Then the bigger fish guided him near to the surface of the river in which they were swimming and said, "If you flip out onto the dry land, you'll soon discover what water is."

These two little stories are parables. The human equivalent is . . . A person ran up to his Christian friend and asked, "Where is this God I hear so much about?"

"He's in you and all about you. You only live because he lives," is the reply.

The prayer of being there for God is a journey towards experiencing this for ourselves.

For me prayer started as a turning to God. It now continues as a turning towards everything else in God. Firstly, I answered the "Come" by looking in one direction. Then the light went out, leaving darkness and silence. Any emergence was not a sudden but, rather, a gradual realisation that this darkness was God, and that this darkness was fertile. From it grew a new way of looking and of living. Now I'm discovering that whatever direction

I look in, it is the same. Once I experienced prayer as a moving from other things towards God. Now I'm beginning to understand that everything else is called towards that movement as well. There is only one movement and only one looking.

Towards integration

The process is now one of bringing together prayer and life. They are not two sides of the same coin; they are closer than that. They are like my daughter's French plait that I mentioned earlier, both strands of God's communication with me, and alike ways of leading me to God. This has come from the darkness. St. Paul says that, "the just shall live by faith" (Hebrews 10:38, Authorised Version); not sight, faith.

The balance of my life has changed. The darkness has dazzled and I'm beginning to see everything else in its light. You know how it is when you stare at the sun. First you can see that light brilliantly, but not a lot else. Then the brilliance starts to take you into itself. The light hurts. You shut your eyes. It's dark but the sun has strung sequins of light on your inner eyelid. The darkness jumps and sparks with light. Then you open your eyes, and the brilliance of the sun is over everything – it dances and specks on fruit or glass; it dapples bushes and grass. It shows up the dust on cars and brings to light the dust in the air around you. Your gazing at the sun has first drawn you from everything else, then it's dazzled you. After that comes the hurt and the blindness. But then the light impinges itself on your inner eye. Finally, you open your eyes cautiously and with a kind of pleased surprise, see everything you look at in that light. You can no longer gaze directly at the source of the light without experiencing a dazzling darkness but it is by that light that everything else is seen. And it's all so much brighter than it was before. Is this what Jesus meant by a fullness of life?

For me faith has not been rewarded by a return to my old seeing, either of God or anything else. Our Father never takes us backwards, always onwards. Faith is moving me deeper into faith (it's a slow process: a dot and carry one limp is about the best spiritual pace I can muster). As I move, I begin to see a lot more around me and within me, in that faith.

Increasingly, I find God speaks to me through people, not through their words but through their quality of life. One of the people who is pointing me very much to God at the moment is a little girl in our church. Her name is Emma, and she's only a few months old. Emma has no hair but she's totally unconcerned by its absence. I suspect she already senses that her eyes are her best feature. Sunday by Sunday I watch those eyes. They've already developed quite a repertoire of seeing. Emma is fascinated by this new world she finds herself in. Her eyes grow round with wonder as they light on red shoes or follow the flute of one of the building's columns right up to the ceiling. It's impossible to love without seeing. I watch as Emma banks away stores of love by her very attentive eyes. She's not learnt deception yet either. She looks at other people with the same intentness. Her look draws you into relationship. She's no longer observing but saying "Hello" with her gaze, just as God does. That's the image of God in her, a seeing that brings relationship, an invitation to love.

An artist friend told me that it can sometimes be difficult to paint animals.

"Why?" I asked.

"Because to paint, you have to observe," he replied.

"What's the problem with that?"

"Animals don't like you looking at them in such a cold way for so long. They don't mind how much you watch them with love or affection. But they find the cold eye of the artist, uninvolved and dissecting, all too much."

"Don't we all?" I muttered to myself.

There's looking and looking. Quite often, I find myself looking without relationship. It's the quick once-over of appraisal – will she do? Is that the right size? Will this face fit? Or else I'm looking to try to draw an object into my own world. Most of the looking of sexual attraction is like that

– it's a chat up of the eyes, and it asks, "How much can I get from you?" Sometimes my looking at my children is like that too. I check they're spruced up and turned out well, and I glow with pride if one of them performs in a play or tootles on solo recorder in school assembly. It's sad if sometimes my glow of pride in them is shot through with flashes of self-congratulation – my children as an extension of my world; their performance a sort of, "And haven't I done well!" to myself.

Seeing is like shot silk. So much depends on the angle at which it is held.

God's angle is different from mine. He always holds his looking up as part of his love. Through his looking relationships develop. From his looking goodness springs. As Genesis says, God looked at creation and saw that it was good. Emma's eyes are still a reflection of that looking. She looks in order to communicate. "Hello," her eyes flash, and then, "I like you." Games are beginning to come into it now. Sometimes she turns quickly and half looks. That's an "Isn't this fun!"

Emma's simplicity is well developed too. What she feels, she communicates. What she thinks, she does. If Emma's had enough of looking and relating, she falls asleep. It's as simple as that. When she's hungry, she cries, then guzzles from her bottle very happily. She is simple because she lives in trust. It doesn't matter if she's not looking. The world will be there next time she opens her eyes. Her looking and her playing and her hunger all take place in the safe confines of her mother's arms. Emma reminds me of Psalm 131:

> O Lord, my heart is not proud,
> nor are my eyes haughty;
> I do not busy myself with great matters
> or things too marvellous for me.
> No; I submit myself, I account myself lowly . . .

Now I'm beginning to experience that God is in everything, life is growing simpler. I don't mean that its demands are fewer. In fact, I'm probably more occupied, and in more areas, than ever before. And what parent with a teenage daughter would ever find the house always peaceful, or life free from surprises and tensions? What I mean is that God is no longer the net to catch me when I fall through life. Life itself, with all its demands and shocks and unpleasantness, is also part of his net. In the darkness, God is setting me free from running to him to escape the world, or from running to religion to escape the reality and demands of my life. One of the best things about this is that I've lost ideals about myself, that picture of a fixed identity which I then have to live up to and, at all costs, protect. Peace is no longer something illusive that I'm always flying to; it is something given by God through what is happening, or not happening, as the case may be. It is not a devil-may-care attitude, but it is a striving which undertakes things, and then leaves the consequences to God. So I act and then don't worry too much about the outcome or other peoples' opinion of what I've done. On good days, that is . . .

Like Emma, simplicity takes whatever's on offer and makes the most of it. When worry and anxiety, the desire to please and the desire to control diminish, energy for love is released. In my teaching, the less I think about how I'm showing up in the situation, the more concern is released for my students' needs; the more flexible my methods, the more imaginative the presentation. God is love because God is one. He is simple: there is no wastage of energy in him. What he thinks, he does; what he dreams, he is; what he wants, he creates. He is also vulnerable, the love never bullies; it allows itself to be rejected. It burns, it pours out, and it is crucified. Its power and its glory lie in this vulnerability.

God is leading me back into the world with a lot more of the barriers between my inner reality and the outer reality melted away. Fewer fantasies, fewer imaginary futures, less of the "if only", make me more available for the now. They also make me more able to connect with it. Part of this connection is learning to act and not to waste energy worrying about the results. Often there'll be mistakes, but the Lord can teach me through these. He can also shield others or teach them from the results of my mistakes.

I hope the Lord will help me to diminish enough to be like Emma. There's a prayer of one of the former Archbishops of Canterbury which puts it in a nutshell. He prayed, "God, who made me simple, make me simpler still." Being simple is not the same as being simplistic. For me, the journey towards even a little more simplicity has taken me through tensions and darkness, away from slick answers and the bandwaggons of the moment. It is still teaching me to trust rather in the generosity of God than in my own responses.

Generosity

Time pleats and, if I fold this February back on last February, I can recall one of God's great kindnesses, a moment when his generosity proved stronger than my weakness. There have been three or four periods of considerable stress in my life, usually months associated with upheaval and new demands which pull me more strongly than I'd bargained for. One of them occurred last February. The foundations of anxiety had been laid for several months. We'd moved house and schools and I'd just started work again.

Body symptoms were telling me loud and clear that I was failing to put my experience into the peace, calm and charity of the Lord.

The first little sense of how much God was strengthening me was that I didn't feel as if I wanted to give up work. In the past it had been all too easy to run from circumstances to God. Now, somehow, I realised God was in the circumstances. They were his invitation to me to learn to cope. Perseverance results in flexibility as well as strength. I felt that if I could hang in long enough, my skills and ability would grow and form to include these new challenges.

Silent waiting on God seemed impossible. I was in too much of a state for that. But one Saturday morning, after the usual night of tossing and turning to dreams twanging with lesson plans and broken or lost equipment, I felt I had to spend my usual time with God or else I'd start to exclude him from the situation. So, with a sigh, and not expecting anything, I stood properly, paying attention to the stretch of my back and the alignment of my head. Thinking that all I had to offer was my anxiety, which seemed a dubious welcome, I stretched out a hand to greet the Lord's presence with me, and started to breathe the Jesus Prayer.

I'd only been standing for a few seconds, was barely conscious of breathing in the Spirit of God, when the anxiety lifted. The joy of the Lord danced in my spirit. It was almost shockingly sudden, a taking up into worship that was quite unexpected. The most I'd tried to do was to connect my situation, the real world with my anxious response to it, to God, his mercy and truth. God had leapt through the tentative connection with the joy of his presence, and the freedom to worship that brings.

Thinking is no longer in opposition to prayer, but it has become more imaginative. My knowledge of God grows not only through prayer but through other people and from reading. God often teaches me not only by reading scripture or specifically Christian books, but from a very broad range of other work, including novels. Scott Fitzgerald wrote a novel called *The Great Gatsby* in which he makes two comments which have illuminated something of human nature for me. Both are echoes of scripture. At one point, the storyteller of the book says of the character Gatsby, "The truth was that Jay Gatsby of West Egg, Long Island, sprang from his Platonic conception of himself. He was a son of God." These words have ushered in months of searching under the Holy Spirit:

How far do I allow God to create and recreate me?
How much effort do I put into continually creating
    myself?

❧

Do I rest in God, or do I form the wife, mother, teacher,
dancer, writer, person I call me?
How much of my life "is hidden with Christ in God", to
use St. Paul's words?

Towards the end of the novel, the storyteller comments
on two of the characters who have created great destruction in the book, "They were careless people ... they
smashed up things and creatures, and then retreated back
into their money or whatever it was that kept them
together." That, too, raises questions for me:

How vast is my carelessness?
What binds me to people? Is it the Spirit of God, or is it
nastier bonds, like the desire to be part of a group, or
to influence others, or to exclude some ... ?

There have been other changes coming from the dark.
When I was first learning how to be there for the Lord in
the prayer of silence, I sometimes went to a convent. The
Sisters there helped me often and showed considerable
patience with my apprentice's lack of perspective. I went
on retreats about twice a year. I owe an enormous debt to
those Sisters. Then, what with young children, my husband's increasing commitments at work which left me the
anchor at home, such luxuries were no longer possible.
Now, I suppose they are, but I don't, for the moment, want
to take advantage of them.

While I prayed during those years when there seemed to
be little response from God, I more than once felt a very
strong inner voice telling me, "If it isn't going to work
here, then it isn't going to work anywhere." For many
people, retreats are part of their preferred rhythm of
living, but I began to feel certain that staying put was the
best I could offer God. Running to a place which would help
evoke religious feelings would, at that time, have been a
form of retreat from God.

Now that the Lord is returning his joy, there doesn't
seem much advantage in going anywhere else to find him.

He's as likely to give me an idea, or to remind me to pray for someone, while I'm peeling the potatoes for supper as he is during Sunday worship. And I'm as likely to be tempted to daydream during prayer group as I am while trying to get some words down on paper.

The years of preparation for prayer and the years when God felt distant seemed to have brought their own gifts. One of the greatest of these is God's generosity. Now, it's not so difficult to slip into his felt presence, however loud the superficial interference is. So the silence wells up when I stop teaching, or the Lord is there in someone speaking to me. Very often, these days, I'm tired when I stop other activities specifically to pray. At first I'm aware only of my exhaustion and heaviness but then the Lord opens his arms. I relax into them and am refreshed by his presence. The grace of God seems always to be leaping towards his creation. He is longing to encourage and woo us and draw us to himself. All we need is to respond a little. The generosity of God takes care of the rest.

A wider love

As we begin to see God in more of the circumstances which confront us – not running from the world to God but reaching out to God in the world, he increases our perseverance, flexibility and concern. We may start to become concerned about things which our upbringing hasn't prepared us for at all. We may also find that the love with which we respond to the world has changed.

I'm often fairly sentimental. Sentimentality is the opposite of love. Nazi sentimentality found it possible to weep over passages in Wagner (the music was so grandly sensitive) and then to condemn thousands to extermination camps. My sentimentality leads to an occasional sigh over the world's starving millions but it doesn't result in a prolonged and sustained concern that puts energy and real slog into working to change conditions. Slog love requires the love of God. Sentimentality turns up at funerals when it has failed to nurse the dying, and sentimentality weeps and gushes at weddings but has bolted when the couple face marital tensions.

Sentimentality plugs the gap when the courage needed to relate has departed. It oozes like syrup and it is just about as nourishing in the long term. Sentimentality urges us to make pets of people.

Jesus was not sentimental, nor was he frightened of the world. He loved it with perseverance and concern. He loved it with the dogged love of God. He loved himself as part of God's world. He respected the rights of others and he respected his own rights too. They were never taken from him, although he finally surrendered them. Jesus was assertive but, because his assertion was rooted in dependence on his Father, even the pleas of friends could not compromise it. Because his love was rooted in God he never needed to be sentimental. He could enable others to face difficult choices in their lives, and he didn't flee from difficult choices in his own life. He faced the reality of the world and the reality of the hearts of men. Above all, Jesus didn't fuss or gush. He penetrated to the centre of a situation and then said or did what was necessary. This meant that sometimes he felt immense sadness and mourning. His love was not always easy; it demanded the best of a person.

When we enter more into the heart of Jesus our love changes; it becomes more like his and this is not always comfortable for ourselves or for others. Some of the most loving people I've come across are not always very cosy to be with. They do not pat me on the head and pet me but they do seek to bring out the best in me. In their company life takes on an exciting aspect. I understand that I was born to fulfil the will of God, which is only another way of saying, I was born to learn how to become as happy and as fully human as possible. They encourage me to want this as well. This is why we find the lives of the saints inspiring. God's love through them urges us on and sometimes in uncomfortable directions. Earlier this week the action of some Christian members of the Peace Movement hit the news headlines. Several of them were arrested when they

tried to daub protest slogans over government build-
ings. They had reckoned that, in this case, breaking the
national law may be a way of bringing the nation's
attention to national injustice.

Love does not exclude anger. Anger against injustice
may become part of our new-found love. A cloying sentimentality about God, ourselves and the world melts away.
It is replaced by something much more robust and whole-
some. It is replaced by love. Love cannot love part of a
person or seek to save part of a life. It cannot indulge in
partial concerns or stand by while the world starves or
threatens to blow itself to bits. That's why, as we move
closer to God, we also become more socially and politically
aware. Jesus is Lord of all creation and so all of the world's
concerns are relevant to our faith. When Mary responded
to the great mercy of God towards her in giving her the
Son, Jesus, her response declared, ". . . he has brought
down monarchs from their thrones" and "The hungry he
has satisfied with good things, the rich sent empty away."
(Luke 1:52–3) When Jesus was executed, the Roman
soldiers tacked up a notice announcing, "Jesus, King of
the Jews". The notice was a statement of political oppres-
sion by Rome over the Jewish people in their occupied
land. God is God of all my life, and God is God of all the
world.

> Spirit of God
> Leap in me
> Dance the dance of your creation
> Your will, not mine, be the song.

12

LOOKING AROUND

We've got two cats: one elderly black mog, very much the
lady, with the most delicate paws I've ever seen. I guess
she thinks so too, for I often catch her looking down at
them with a concentrated gaze which seems suspiciously
close to appreciation. The other animal is a young Turk, a
Persian of three years old, soft, stupid, relaxed and
lumbering. He was dubbed "Parsley" before he came to us.
He's a cat of large paws, remarkably little brain but of one
obsession. He loves eating heart. He seems to have a sixth
sense which operates as soon as I prise a solid lump from
the freezer. Although it's left to thaw out well beyond his
reach, he makes pilgrimages to the larder door at frequent
intervals and stands there, scenting the rate of progress.
Even if he's asleep when the actual meal time arrives, his
sixth sense wakes him to full alert in two shakes of a cat's
whisker. No sooner have I got the scissors out of the
drawer to cut the meat, than he's there, weaving round my
legs, pleading and mewing for the first delicious morsel.
I've not been able to work out how he knows it's the
scissors I've taken from the drawer. He's there before he
can have seen them. There's complete indifference if I'm
looking for the cat knife to chop up his normal tinned food.
As the bowl fills with heart, every fibre of his body quivers
to red alert. His great round eyes glisten with adoration,
his ears twitch, his whiskers stand to attention and the
fluffy hairs on his cheeks almost rustle in anticipation.

On non-heart days he goes about his own business,
grubbing round the garden, sitting on the fence, best
profile to the road (this started after he'd picked up snip-
pets of conversation about the nobility of the lions in *Out of
Africa*) or sleeping for hours, nose pressed to the radiator.

Even so, occasionally, there's a twitch through his dreams
or a misty look in those amber eyes which could be the
memory of the last heart supper, or even a dream of the
next . . . To sum it up, this cat's life revolves round heart.
When heart calls, everything else is forgotten. Heart also
seems to underlie the rest of his activities in a curious way,
like a tug deep down which pulls the whole of his life in
that direction.

As Christians we can sometimes feel a little confused
about loving God and loving anything else. Perhaps we
could learn something from this rather stupid Persian cat.
He's got lots of things he appreciates: tickles round the
ears, a warm radiator, chasing birds, dozing in the sun-
light, but when heart calls, he drops everything in a flash
to respond immediately. He also distinguishes between
the call of heart and other things. That comes from experience of heart days. I suspect, although I can't prove it, that
the experience of heart sometimes surprises him at times
when he least expects it.

What can this tell us about our life in God? Perhaps it
indicates we were born to enjoy great diversity. All that
the Lord asks is that when we hear his call, we answer
quickly and with expectation just as Parsley responds to
the first indication that heart's on the menu. Perhaps we
can develop a sense of when the Lord's going to call and
start to prepare ourselves (the equivalent of checking on
the larder door from time to time). The cat doesn't bother
to run for anything except heart. That's a bit more difficult. We need practice to learn to discern God's voice, to
see only God. We learn through experience. As we come to
the Lord again and again, we begin to know what he's like
and a little of how he thinks. Then, when we feel he's
calling, we're quick to discern what is him and what isn't.

Parsley doesn't spend all his time thinking about heart
or waiting for it to appear. He seems secure in the knowledge that, some time, it will be served up again. As we grow
in prayer, we grow in the knowledge that it is not we who
have to catch God but it is God, our Father, who has
already caught us and holds us in his arms. There's no risk

that we can fall through his fingers. There's no fear that other loves can take us from the love of God. We start to experience that all love comes from God, and we are released to enjoy so much in God's world. When I was first aware of the presence of God I worried that loving my husband might diminish my love for God. Now I understand how babyish such a fear was. All good gifts come from God, and once the centre of our life has settled into him, his generosity showers us with his goodness. It's a spiritual law: meanness breeds more meanness; fear more fear; but also, joy leads to increasing joy and love to increasing love. There is a distinction between God and his gifts, but there's not a distinction between loving God and loving his creation. What artist isn't delighted when you compliment him on his work of art? It doesn't make sense to say, "How wonderfully you paint!" and to follow it with, "But I really can't afford to like your paintings." Love wastes itself, and the more it lavishes itself on God, the less it fears that lavishing itself on anything else will threaten God. All my relationships are ways by which the Lord leads me to himself. My approach to God's gifts is somewhat simpler now. It takes the form of a heartfelt "Thank you."

We are still left with Parsley's seeming preoccupation with heart. This, too, is a theme which runs through God's creation. When I'm called to think, I think as hard as possible, or when to act, the same. However, when there's nothing specific to be done, or when housework isn't calling for any great brain power, then my spirit has a preoccupation. Words of scripture pop into my mind to be mulled over or, with a flash of insight, to sparkle with deeper clarity. Perhaps there's a pull towards someone or some situation in prayer. More often than not, it's just a sense of the presence of God or the step from a rather small, specific concern to the larger world of God's here and now – that landscape of joy and sorrow, peopled with angels and archangels and the glorious company of Heaven, as well as those whose response to God, like mine, is not yet complete.

A growing silence

It's as if silence spreads, like a pool, under the activity of
my life. Whenever activity ceases, God's Spirit calls me
back into this silence which is the voice of God for me.
Then I'm teaching, and in the breath before the students
enter, I hold them before God; or it's Saturday morning
and after the scramble of family breakfast and in the
bustle of town, the silence empties into prayer for someone
at church or for a political prisoner on the other side of the
world. The car's at traffic lights and I catch the anxiety on
the face of the driver drawn up next to me; that's dropped
into God's love. This isn't a conscious turning to God. It's a
kind of undertow in my life, as natural as breathing and at
its best when the silence isn't emptied into immediate
concerns, even the concern of prayer for others. At best, it's
nothing more than a resting in God. Like breathing, I only
notice it when there's a difficulty. If you're out of breath
then gasping reminds you how important that regular IN
and OUT is in your life. If the undertow of silence goes
(frightened away by me) then I'm equally breathless, half
alive, gasping for the love of God in which to sink my
activity. God has developed as a sort of home. If I wander
too far away, then the long ache of homesickness pulls me
back.

Prayer in the world

This is God's world, and God speaks to us through it. The
material world, the world I touch, smell, see, hear and
taste is often how God communicates with me. The God
who showed his love through a flesh and blood person still
speaks through a hand on mine, or a smile and a listening
ear. The God who chose an ordinary woman's womb in
which to become that person, comes to me through ordinary people and through all this world, not just the obviously beautiful. For some people the response to natural
beauty is very strong. A friend told me the other day, "I
can't live without trees." And added, "I can't pray without

them." Her need was so strong that, when she lost all the mature trees in the garden in the great October storm, she immediately went out and bought eight new saplings to plant in their place. "I know," she went on, "I ought to work on growing trees in my heart so that I can pray anytime." I'm not so sure. We're not disembodied spirits but part of God's physical creation. Perhaps all she and I and each one of us needs to do is to see God in everything he has made and not just in what naturally attracts us. There are more scrubby tufts of grass around than trees; when I find those beautiful, I have more reminders of God's beauty and care. Perhaps this is why Jesus chose the stuff of everyday life, bread and wine, to be our remembrance of him. Their very ordinariness is a reminder of the holiness of everything else we call ordinary.

As we grow towards God, we see him in more and more, and we see more and more in him. For God there is no sacred and secular. Everything is made to praise him. Cleaning the house to his glory or working on the computer are akin to preaching a sermon or praying a prayer. As we learn to live in our true environment where everything is seen in God and where we move under his loving gaze, we experience more and more connections. The world takes on relationships; it becomes a "you" not an "it". We may be less sentimental about flowers or animals, nevertheless we may start to say "Hello" to them. One of the Christians who was most aware of the interconnectedness of all God's world was St. Francis, and he ended up doing just that. When the Kingdom of God becomes formed in a person, then the Kingdom is extended to the air, the creatures and the vegetation around that person, as well as to other people. We are led by the Spirit into love, and those nearest God sense friendship from such unlikely sources as reptiles and insects. Everything in creation is part of a song of praise to the Creator. Everything is a brother or a sister. Everything asks for a "Hello" and is willing to give a "Hello" back. Everything that we touch, taste, see, handle or hear is destined to find its pleasure in God. We eat the bread and we drink the

wine at communion in order to understand that all bread
and all wine, all God's material world, is waiting to shine
with his glory if we will but look at it in his love. Contemplation starts by turning from the world to gaze at God in
love. Then it learns that God's gaze is everywhere. It
progresses by turning an alert and reverent gaze back on
the world as an invitation to enter into love. God invites
us, and God in the world invites us. As we respond to these
invitations in their various forms, so our joy increases.

The body of love

Sometimes I think we change physically too. I've met at
least two people who, by their bodily presence alone, have
spoken to me of God. They were both so at home in God, in
his world and in themselves that, physically, they moved
like a parable. Their movement was, for me, far more
powerful than words. Come to think of it, I didn't even
speak to one of them. This was a youngish man whom I
noticed at one of our church services several years ago. He
was quite tall and stood out above the heads of most of the
congregation when we got up to sing a hymn. At the end of
the hymn, the minister moved to the pulpit in order to
start his sermon. We sat down. No, we didn't. We shuffled
and sat; we wriggled and slouched; we pulled out handker-
chieves; twiddled thumbs or thrutched back against the
pew, trying to get comfortable. Some people crossed and
then uncrossed their legs. I smoothed down my skirt; an
older man, next but one to me, started to tap his foot on the
floor. But the young man sat. In one graceful, co-ordinated
movement, he lowered himself from standing to sitting.
Once sitting, he didn't move again but his back spoke of a
relaxed alertness that meant he was ready to listen to the
sermon and to look at what was going on in the church. His
back seemed to me to be part of his listening and looking,
at once receptive and ready and present in a way that
made the rest of us appear preoccupied, disconnected and
inattentive.
    The second person whose movement spoke to me of the

work of God in her body, was a Sister I glimpsed for only about thirty seconds at the convent where I used to go for quiet days. She was from India and when I saw her she was loading some coal from a stockpile into a bucket with a shovel. She had her back turned to me, and as I came out of the guest house she must have heard the click of the door shutting behind me. She didn't turn or pause in the rhythm of her loading. The Sisters train themselves to be present to whatever they are doing. They don't leak their energy into curiosity about things they are not doing at that moment. She bent and loaded with a graceful swinging action. But I wanted to interrupt her. I didn't know the way to the library from the guest house and needed a book for some work I was doing. "Excuse me, Sister," I began softly, standing just behind her.

At once she turned to me, bucket in hand, smiling. Again I felt that strong sense of being present. Without strain, she had moved from the concerns of loading the coal to the concerns of a person. I was not an interruption to her, but felt very much part of God's world for her, a part which, at that particular moment, wanted her attention. Her smile was very encouraging. I asked the way to the library.

In a gentle voice, she told me, "Go into the house and turn right. At the end of the corridor you'll come to some stairs. If you go up them, you'll see the library door directly ahead of you at the top."

The words couldn't have been more ordinary. But she might have been reading scripture for the care and the warmth she put into them. They were spoken completely without fuss, nor did she move her hands to emphasise what she was saying. When she'd finished and seen that I'd taken in the instructions she turned back to the coal and began shovelling again. Just as with the young man in the church, I was struck with the quality of her presence. She was attentive, whether it was to the coal or to me. Her attentiveness spoke of an integration within herself, a simplicity that, whatever it was doing, was waiting on God.

204 JOURNEY OF PRAYER

Sometimes I wonder how Jesus moved; how much he talked with his body. St. Luke tells us, "As Jesus grew up he advanced in wisdom and in favour with God and men." (Luke 1:52) The position of the two comments next to each other interests me. Perhaps his everyday growth was favourable and perhaps his body had about it, even in everyday situations, that grace and singleness that was to shine out so brightly at the Transfiguration. We see the luminosity of God fully in Jesus but, for me, to a lesser degree, it was also present in the man in church and the Sister in her convent. Bodily grace and simplicity are the result of being present to God and present to everything else in God without trying to control or to judge. Such presence is the body of love.

Possession

What do I mean by talking about not trying to control? It's soon obvious to anyone who tries to catch the wind that he can't. But at first, it wasn't obvious to me that I couldn't catch and hang on to other people, or my moods, or snow-drops or the animals I call my pets. Everything and everyone has its own life in God. My journey towards God has been a journey of "hands off". Whenever I try to possess, something dies; or rather, I start to kill it. I also kill my true self. Possession isolates and often disappoints.

I can remember a time when I longed for a model pony about 8 inches long, covered with real pony skin. I must have been about ten years old. I dreamed of the thing, daily pressed my nose to the glass of the shop window where it was on display, pestered my mother and saved every bit of pocket money. At last came the wonderful day when I could buy it. I hopped from foot to foot with impatience as the assistant drew it from the window and wrapped it. She seemed to take hours to fold the paper. Then, I lovingly cradled it in my arms. Right away, one of its hind legs stabbed my bare wrist, through the paper. I got it home, unwrapped it and looked at it. I don't know what I hoped for – perhaps, that if I looked enough, I'd look it into life. It didn't change. I stroked it. A sickening emptiness began to creep into my stomach. What next? The emptiness congealed into a lump like cold porridge. All the waiting and the hoping; all the love, had brought me – what? A rather hard, misshapen model. I'd thought you could buy dreams, and by the age of ten, had my first lesson on the impossibility of that.

Now I'm older, I've found out it's the same with all sorts of things, including people. Once I fight for something as "mine" I've forfeited the mystery of that particular life. I've stopped relating and my true self dies a little. Jesus told us quite clearly, "Be on your guard against greed of every kind, for even when a man has more than enough, his wealth does not give him life." (Luke 12:15) We can be greedy for more than money; for people and ideas; for ideals and influence; for our own thoughts and feelings.

The Holy Spirit is beginning to show me that I don't possess my experience of God. For me, reflection on prayer (and hasn't the whole of this book been just that?) is one of the last greeds that I'm willing to let go. As long as my peace and joy and love remain my possession, they remain prey to my moods and circumstances. If I allow God to hold them, I start to understand that they are taken care of by much more caring hands than mine. Everything is given, and everything is valuable. I once heard quite a young bishop talking about the givenness of life. He said he hoped to learn to practise laying everything on an open palm before God. "But what about dying?" someone asked him.

"If I learn not to possess," the bishop answered quietly, "then my life won't be mine. So, when the time comes, I hope I'll hardly notice."

> Lord of freedom and joy
> Help us to leave everything for you
> And then help us to enjoy everything
> Because of you.

13

REACHING HOME

One long, hot summer, when I was eleven years old, my parents loaded me into our old family car and drove me sixty miles from our house to drop me at a camp. The leaders there were most welcoming and the other girls very nice but I was miserable. Home, for me, was where my parents were. Each day I clambered on to one of the stone lions that guarded some steps in the beautiful grounds of the school where we were staying. Astride the back of the lion, I gazed out and away, across the glistening estuary of the River Dee back to my home. It was the only comfort I had, a looking that leapt the distance and pleated the time between me and what I loved. Beneath me, the patient, stone, lichen encrusted lion sat solid. The warm solidity of his back did its bit to give me just a toe hold of security in all that abandonment.

As an adult, I'm learning to interpret all my deepest longings as just such a home sickness. We say that we come from God and that we're going to God. That's just another way of saying God is our home.

In contemplation, the prayer of looking at God, we leap distance and we pleat time.

We leap distance

God whispers that he is everywhere. We turn to look at him, and he turns us to look at his world. In contemplation we stand as a bridge between God and his world. We look both ways but we see with the same eyes. We soon discover we are looking with the same love. Wherever we look, we are looking in God; whatever is seen is given by God. So, all our journeying has taken us nowhere. There was

nowhere to go. There was only the response to the call
"Come," and then to see everything that was there before.
But to see it as new. We behold just a little of the beauty of
the Lord and that beauty dazzles us for life. Its sparkle
shines on everything we see. It is as Jesus has declared,
"Behold, I am making all things new."

Amen, Lord. And in your continual coming, lead me
further into your new life.

We pleat time

Time was created by God. As we move into God, so our life
in time is reconciled to his life in eternity. Our coming to
God brings us into a new understanding of time.

The past is ours. As St. Paul declared, "In Christ he
[God] chose us before the world was founded." (Ephesians
1:4) We begin to feel our links with the past. Perhaps we
feel them first in our own lives; past suffering healed in
God. Years ago I retravelled the years to the isolation of
the eleven-year-old child astride her lion. I relived the
scene, this time with the love of God surrounding me. As a
Christian I know that there is no part of my past life in
which the Lord has not been a net under me.

We may also experience past sin brought to light and
forgiven.

Then we move to a wider past with prayer for our
country's history, when we stand as a bridge between the
mercy of God and distant national injustice.

As we experience all of creation in God, then we may
develop a sense of continuity with the past of this creation.
We look up into the night sky or we run the palm of our
hand over ancient, granite rocks at the sea side, and we
know that connections are made in God between everything, even between the creation before man and our
present selves. Here we are entering the territory of the
Psalmist:

When I look up at thy heavens, the work of thy fingers,
the moon and the stars set in their place by thee,

what is man that thou shouldst remember him,
mortal man that thou shouldst care for him?

$$\text{(Psalm 8:3–4)}$$

Part of living in the new creation is inviting the old creation into this new wholeness. We are the present links in a long chain of life and a great variety of form. Our prayer is midwife to the birth of the old order into the new. We are both guardians and celebrators of all life.

The future is ours. The future finds its fulfilment in God. As St. Paul says of the resurrection at the end of time, ". . . God will be all in all." (1 Corinthians 15:28) Jesus healed relationships, he forgave sins, he brought peace to people and to angry waves, he enriched water into wine, he healed, he raised the dead – all to indicate the abundant life of God. We catch flashes of that life now as we live in God. Every sinner who repents, every person who is healed physically or emotionally, every relationship renewed, every life of worship, every person celebrated is a present indication of the future. When God is all in all, then that abundance of life, the life which swallows death in all its forms, will be our normal life. We are now being changed from glory to glory. In the future we shall inhabit God's glory as our home, because his grace will have enabled us to do so. "Now we see only puzzling reflections in a mirror, but then we shall see face to face." (1 Corinthians 13:12) Now we live a partial life, then the partial will vanish when wholeness comes.

Very recently, I experienced a couple of instances of this future wholeness bursting through the partial present and, for a moment, bringing with them the vividness of God's life. The first of these was our church pantomime. For a start, it was a home grown production, written, directed and put on by church members. There were lead parts but no prima donnas, and the chorus of singers and dancers provided much more than background. Maybe that's because I recognised everyone in the erratically waving line. There was a lot of laughter, jokes at piety and the sometimes irksome, if necessary structures of parish life. The cast helped each other, admired each other, and enjoyed each other. The warmth of the relationships forged by working together are still felt when we meet together for eucharist Sunday by Sunday, now several weeks later.

Such bonds of community are a sign of the fuller community of Heaven. Then we shall celebrate each other eternally. We shall live in enjoyment as God lives in enjoyment. We shall be like him because, as St. John explains, ". . . we shall see him as he is." (1 John 3:2) We shall become full expressions of the life of God. The fire of his love will have burned our hearts into its own leaping flames. In Heaven we will not compete with each other. Our love will be so great that there will be no distinction between giving and receiving. Everyone will be necessary and no one will be left out. All our giving and taking, all our enjoyment of each other, will be part of our song of praise and of our Father's joy in us.

The second instance you may have heard about on the News when, earlier this year, the Archbishop of Canterbury sent one of his bishops to South Africa to stand beside Desmond Tutu in his cry for freedom in that country. The English bishop did just that, literally, in front of the cameras. And, as he did so, he announced, "If you hit one of us, you hit us all." Those are prophetic words. They tell forth the Lord's understanding of his Church as a body. They tell forth the sympathy, empathy, solidarity of concern that is beyond race or culture or sex or class. They are the modern equivalent of St. Paul's great cry of freedom, "There is no such thing as Jew and Greek, slave and freeman, male and female; for you are all one person in Christ Jesus." (Galatians 3:28) Such acts point to the coming of the Kingdom of God in its fullness.

We live in the now. Above all, for each one of us, it is the present that we must lift to God's eternity. Or, to put it another way, it is God who does the lifting. Through his prophet Joel he declared that he would pour out his Spirit on all mankind; not just on his named people but on all mankind. (Joel 2:28) The person who prays lives where eternity is continually pouring itself into time. It's the job of each person who lives before the Lord to discover God in each moment. It is in God in whom we live and move, and in whom we exist. God is always seeking to lift his world into this awareness.

Not long ago, I heard of a girl in Sweden, a punk girl in black leather with spikey hair and studded jewellery. She was walking along a road one Sunday, idling her way around the hollow of the morning when, on impulse, she turned into a church where an Englishman was speaking at the service. He noticed her at the back: she stood out dramatically from the neatly dressed normal church-goers. But she left quickly at the end of the service before he had a chance to speak to her. She rang the house where he was staying late that afternoon and explained, "I just felt I had to come in. All the time I was in the service I felt myself full of speech, not ordinary language but a foreign language that welled up in me. I held it in while I was in church but I've been speaking it ever since. It sounds like this . . ." She spoke in tongues down the phone. "I feel really, really happy. What's happening?"

What's happening is that God is sweeping his uncaring world into his own ever-caring presence. He is fulfilling something of what Joel told us about his Spirit falling on all people.

A continuing journey

Everything and everyone is alive in God. Because they are alive only in God, everything and everyone is connected. The Holy Spirit is continually winging these connections through the universe. In prayer, we become more aware of these connections. An unseen gesture of love makes a grid for God's power to release itself. My task in prayer is continually to realise these connections at deeper and deeper levels and so, to release more of God's loving power into his creation.

To do this I stand as a bridge, firstly between God and

myself, over which his love and graciousness flow to me, always finding new levels of darkness in me to woo into his marvellous light. Then I stand as a bridge between God and all of my life. As God gives himself to me in prayer, I start to understand that everything in my life is part of this givenness. Nothing is held: everything is gift; everything is celebrated, and everything passes. It is God who guards my life, not I. Prayer is the mustard seed of worship from which worship spreads into all of my life. Ultimately, drinking a cup of tea or telling a prophecy; filing some old papers or exercising discernment are, alike, acts of worship. So, I move from cooking a casserole to the glory of God, to dancing in his joy, from working in his energy, to lying flat in awe of his holiness. Or, I wish I did! I am not yet able to say like St. Paul, "whether we live or whether we die, it is to the Lord." My grasp on myself – my thoughts, my feelings, my preferences, my anxieties – is still very strong. But the God whose arms have held and guided and beckoned and enfolded so far, will, by his Spirit, continue to ease my fingers further into his own. My job is merely to be present to him: to answer his "Come" with "Here I am". Like Jesus I need to come again and again and again until I can learn to stand more firmly and to look at everything in wonder and in awe.

Finally, I stand as a bridge between God and his world, the world which, in him, is always sacred.

The journey of prayer does not seem to me to be a straight line, starting at a beginning and continuing without break or kink towards some sort of perfection. I experience the journey in a shape more like that of a spiral, taking me to new levels with each turn, and retreading old ground in a different way each time.

Prayer is a constant surprise, and I am a constant amateur.

So it seems that reaching home is going nowhere. Reaching home is that continual travelling further on and further into the reality of who God is; of who I am; and of the world in which I live. It is to be shot through with longing, and yet threaded by peace.

Reaching home is receiving my life as God's gift
Reaching home is learning to be present to God in
   God's world
It is realising connections, and then being educated
   into gladness
Reaching home is thirsting for God and for justice
It is learning to live with attention
Reaching home is being so much in this moment, here
   and now, that I take this moment into God
Reaching home is living in you, Lord.

And what is needed for this? Only two things. One I am
sure of, and that is the mercy of God. For the mercy of God
has folded itself under and around my life; the mercy of
God holds strong arms over and about me. The mercy of
God moves me on.

The other thing? The other I'm not so sure of. It seems
that all I need to respond to God's mercy, to run into his
arms in and through his world, is humility. And that's a
trickier question . . .

> And so, Lord God, of our mercy,
> Call me to you
> Hold me in you
> Unfold yourself in me
> Until, Lord God, I awake with your likeness.

A JOURNEY INTO GOD

Delia Smith

'Anyone who lives, prays, for prayer is that deeper level of human existence which we call the spiritual life. The journey of prayer is nothing more nor less than a gradual awakening to the reality of recognising what is already there.'

As a communicator, Delia Smith has always been motivated by a need, whether for clear explanation of the basic skills of cooking, or, as in this book, for a simple presentation of the meaning of prayer. Writing with clarity and wisdom on a subject of deep personal significance, Delia Smith's daily readings draw on a wide range of writings, as well as her own experience of 'the journey into God'. Here is a simple but profound guide for ordinary people seeking a deeper knowledge of God.

'. . . a useful and practical guide: she is as trustworthy when it comes to the spiritual life as she is in the kitchen.'
The Sunday Times

'For someone who prays, it is like having a wise, practical friend on the same wavelength.'
Lionel Blue

'This is a magnificent book for anyone who wants to pray. A spiritual classic for today.'
David Konstant, Bishop of Leeds

ALL THE DAYS OF MY LIFE

Penelope Flint

'I admire the skill and innate wisdom with which she interweaves the real with the more-than-real. She has managed to give another dimension to the problems that beset our age. God knows we need a perspective such as hers.'

Mary Craig

Written during her third pregnancy, *All the Days of My Life* is a profound autobiography of originality and charm in which Penelope Flint's own growing spiritual awareness mirrors the growth of the child within. It culminates in the seventh month of pregnancy, with her acceptance as an external candidate to St Mary's Convent, Wantage – a symbolic confirmation of an inner process which had begun in her days studying English at Oxford.

Interspersed with Penelope Flint's own startling poetry, *All the Days of My Life* is a vivid account of the inner and outer life of a woman searching for an authentic spiritual reality. It affirms that space for reflection and growth can and must be found amidst the pressures of everyday life. The author's knowledge of philosophical and Christian writings, and her understanding of current affairs, enhance this outstanding book.